ESSAYS ON TEACHING AND LEARNING

by

Dr. MARLOW EDIGER
Emeritus Professor of Education
Truman State University
P.O. Box 417, 201 W 22nd St
North Newton KS 67117
United States of America

and

Dr. DIGUMARTI BHASKARA RAO
Reader and Research Director
R.V.R. College of Education
D-43 (277) S.V.N. Colony
Guntur-522006, India

DISCOVERY PUBLISHING HOUSE PVT. LTD.
NEW DELHI-110 002

Published by:
Tilak Wasan

DISCOVERY PUBLISHING HOUSE PVT. LTD.
4831/24, Prahlad Street, Ansari Road
Darya Ganj, New Delhi-110002 (India)
Phone: +91-11-23279245, 43764432
Fax: +91-11-23253475
E-mail: parul.wasan@gmail.com
discoverypublishinghouse@gmail.com
info@discoverypublishinggroup.com
web: www.discoverypublishinggroup.com

***First Edition:* 2011**
ISBN: 978-81-8356-879-1

Printed at:
Shree Balaji Art Press
Delhi

dedicated
to

Dr. Kondabolu Basava Punnaiah
President
J.K.C. College
R.V.R. & J.C. College of Engineering
R.V.R. College of Education
College of Nursing
C.H. Institute of Pharmaceutical Sciences
Dr. K.L.P. Public School

Preface

Education is that act or experience which has a formative effect on the mind, character or physical ability of an individual. Education is also the process by which society deliberately transmits its accumulated knowledge, skills and values from one generation to another. Education is imparted through teaching and learning. Teaching refers to the actions of a real live instructor designed to impart learning to the student. Learning refers to learning with a view toward preparing learners with specific knowledge, skills, or abilities that can be applied immediately upon completion.

Teachers in the educational institutions direct the education of students and draw on many subjects, including languages, mathematics, science and social studies. This process is called the teaching and learning, which involves both the teachers and the students in realizing the set objectives. The teachers and administrators need to know several aspects related to teaching and learning, which make them the best in their fields.

The book entitled **Essays on Teaching and Learning** provides various means and modes to improve the teaching and learning. This book will be of great use to school teachers and school administrators.

Digumarti Bhaskara Rao
digumartibhaskararao@redeiffmail.com

Sri Sai Soudha
D-43 S.V.N. Colony
Guntur 522006
India

Contents

1

CHAPTER

Principal and Teaching and Learning Process

Today's school principal has a plethora of duties and responsibilities. Among many others, he/she is expected to supervise and monitor teacher progress in the classroom. Too frequently in the past, principals performed largely management duties in schools, but now each principal must also assist in teaching and learning situations. How might the principal be of service to assist teachers in improving the curriculum?

The Principal as Supervisor in the Curriculum

To do well in supervision, the principal must develop good rapport with classroom teachers. Hostility and mistrust have no role to play when developing a quality curriculum. Negative attitudes toward others hinders interactions among the principal and teachers. A feeling of acceptance needs to be in the offing. The school climate needs to emphasize politeness, feelings of belonging, and honest praise for quality work performed. The latter helps individuals to meet esteem needs. Too often, teachers and principals come to school each day of the calendar year with little or no attention being given to that which is done well by any one individual. The routiness of these situations must be broken to bring in a school climate which encourages and welcomes faculty members as well as support personnel (Ediger, 2007a&b).

This sets the stage then for principals and teachers working together to develop the best curriculum possible for students. The stated objectives for pupils to achieve must be attainable. If the mandated objectives are too rigid and complex, the principal may assist teachers to develop enabling objectives which help pupils to achieve the desired end. These enabling objectives assist pupils to sequentially realize the original complex goal. Another approach for assisting teachers in teaching is for the principal to stress the concept of scaffolding. Thus, for example, the objective is too difficult for pupils to attain. However with scaffolding, pupils are aided with a series of sequentially arranged learning activities to realize the complex objective or goal. Thus, there are definite strategies for aiding pupils to achieve difficult learnings, either through enabling objectives or through scaffolding. The principal needs to guide teachers to study these two concepts in depth. Then too, the principal may use demonstration teaching to show how to put these two and other strategies into operation. When classroom teachers use either or both procedures, they need to report back to school professionals what they did to implement and how they felt the new procedures affected pupil achievement (Ediger, 2007a&b).

Teachers may need assistance in stressing knowledge (knowing about enabling objectives and scaffolding), as well as skills objectives (strategies to use in implementing the acquired knowledge in teaching and learning situations). Attitudes as objectives result from learning experiences involving knowledge and skills ends. If the following occur during teaching and learning situations, the chances are negative attitudes have been developed :

- excess drill which takes the joy out of the ongoing experiences

- pressure to achieve beyond what the learner can possibly attain.
- a lack of challenge.
- dull learning activities.
- inadequate explanations given within the learning activity (Ediger, 2008a&b).

Alignment of Learning Activities

School principals must guide teachers to align learning experiences with the stated objectives. Learning activities need to be aligned with the chosen objectives to optimize pupil achievement. The objectives provide direction for changes to be made within the learner. The learning activities assist in bringing about the necessary modifications. Too frequently, the objectives have been stated too broadly and thus provide little help in knowing what the objective means. The other extreme is to write objectives which are too specific, resulting in facts, only, being taught. Thus, a happy medium must be sought whereby objectives are specific enough to agree upon what will be taught and, at the same time, possess adequate leeway to provide for higher cognitive levels of subject matter being taught such as critical and creative thinking as well as problem solving (Guilfoyle, 2006).

School principals need to help teachers choose learning activities which are varied to develop and maintain learner interests. Reading experiences, audio visual aids, discussions, small and large group work, as well as the integration of technology need to be incorporated into the curriculum. Individual differences must be provided for including interest differences, diverse learning styles, and multiple intelligences. Teachers must assist pupils to develop :

- quality self-concepts whereby there is confidence for achieving.
- feelings of curiosity in knowledge and skills being taught.

- habits of being responsible for objectives to be attained.
- traits of friendliness in learning to accept each pupil in the classroom and school.
- polite behavior avoiding rudeness, and negative judgemental statements made about others (Ediger, 2008a&b).

A school climate needs to emerge which encourages optimal student learning. This implies, too, that the environment for learning encourages quality teaching. Learners need to feel respected in a relaxed environment for learning. Pupils must be actively engaged in learning. Interest needs to be a major factor in teaching pupils in securing their attention. Any learning experience may be made interesting with appropriate selections made. Methods used along with the learning experience must be varied such as using inductive, deductive, problem solving, textbook, multi-media, and project method approaches. Principals should assist teachers to guide pupils to perceive purpose for learning. Thus, learners are assisted to perceive reasons for achieving objectives of instruction. Facts, concepts, and generalizations taught and achieved need to be meaningful. They must be understood by pupils since each becomes a building block for ensuing activities. Quality sequence stresses that pupils are able to relate previous with subsequent subject matter. A good school climate then emphasizes providing for individual differences in an environment conducive to learning (Tighe and O'Conner, 2005).

Grouping Pupils for Instruction

Each principal needs to have good understanding ways of grouping learners for instructional purposes. Placing pupils into groups is not done for the sake of grouping, but rather to assist learners to achieve well. There are a plethora of means of placing pupils into groups to advance achievement for each. If, for example, individualized reading is being stressed, then no groups need be formed. In a nutshell, Each pupil selects a library book to read of his/her choosing and then have a conference with the teacher to appraise achievement after its reading. Also, a one on one conference may be conducted with the teacher and an involved pupil to discuss a learning strategy. Or, the short discussion may help the pupil in a followup writing activity. The conference may be held at the pupil's own desk. Motivating pupils in achieving is always important (Maslow, 1954).

A small group may be formed when three or four pupils have read the same paperback and discuss it contents in a peer committee setting. Standards need to be followed by peer members so that each might do well in the classroom setting. There are times, too, when peer teaching may be stressed. A peer may do well in assisting learners in word attack skills. There is a purpose, here, in using peer teaching and that being a peer's proficiency in helping others in instructional situations (Cai, 2008).

Small groups may be formed by the teacher to teach an advanced set of achievers. These learners are progressing satisfactorily at a more rapid rate than others in the classroom.

What has been diagnosed as being a common problem to a given set of learners might well also provide for small group instruction. The problem may pertain to :

- use of context clues in reading
- reading critically, creatively, and/or to solve problems
- the pupil monitoring his/her own reading achievement
- reflecting over what has been read
- specific difficulties in using phonics (Bloodgood and Pacific, 2004).

Small groups may also be used in clarifying what was presented in large group instruction. When large groups are used to initiate a lesson or unit plan of teaching, then questions will arise which can be handled in smaller group settings.

The grouping plan used must meet the needs of involved learners. The plan implemented is to assist pupils to achieve more optimally. There is a purpose inherent in developing each grouping plan. Adequate supervision must be used in each plan. The school principal needs to assist teachers to think through as to which plan of grouping will help learners to achieve more optimally under the circumstances in the school and classroom settings.

Inservice Education

What role does the principal play in inservice teacher education? There is a vital purpose in having inservice education. Teachers need to upgrade knowledge and skills in teaching. New developments, philosophies, theories, and research result in reassessing what is presently being emphasized in the curriculum. Thus, a need for inservice education is necessary.

A survey may be conducted to notice teacher needs in improving the curriculum. This might result in adopting a completely new programme in teaching whereby inservice is needed to become thoroughly familiar with its adopting its methodology en toto, including objectives, learning opportunities, and evaluation procedures. A series of meetings are then conducted to implement the new curriculum. Otherwise, there may be specifics which teachers might like to experience within inservice education. These might well include the following :

- using scripted procedures of teaching, such as Open Courts reading series
- using work book activities to supplement the basal in guiding student progress
- using creative dramatics to breath life into content read
- building background knowledge within pupils for the ensuing reading experience

- assisting students to predict what will transpire in a subsequent reading selection
- helping students to reflect upon what has been read
- engaging in inferential reading
- engaging students in using internet sources (Van Horn, 2007).

The principal needs to inform teachers to feel a need for inservice education programmes. Important concepts and generalizations acquired in a workshop need to be tried out in the classroom to notice its affects upon students. These affects need to be reported back to participants in the workshop. Ideas from the workshop need to circulate among participants in a question and answer session. Openess to new ideas in teaching must be encouraged! The total workshop must be evaluated in terms of recommended criteria and should pinpoint items such as relevance to improving instruction, importance in meeting pupil needs in the classroom, and stressing salient principles of psychology in teaching and learning.

References

Bloodgood, Janet, and Linda C. Pacific (2004), "Bringing Word Study to Intermediate Classrooms," *The Reading Teacher*, 58 (3), 250-265.

Cal, Mingshui (2008), "Transaction Theory and the Study of Multicultural Literature" *Language Arts*, 85 (3), 212-220.

Ediger, Marlow (2007a), "Learning Activities Across the Curriculum," *College Student Journal*, 41 (4), 967-969.

Ediger, Marlow (2007b), "Meaning in Reading Instruction," *Reading Improvement*, 44 (4), 217-220.

Ediger, Marlow (2008a), "Mental Health and the Curriculum," *Journal of Instructional Psychology*, 35 (1), 38-42.

Ediger, Marlow (2008a), "Leadership in the School Setting," Education, 129(1), 17-20.

Guilfoyle, Christy (2006), "NCLB : Is There Life After Testing?," *Educational Leadership*, 64 (3), 8-14.

Maslow, A. H. (1954), *Motivation and Personality*, New York : Harper and Row.

Tighe, Jay, and Ken O'Conner (2005), "Seven Practices for Effective Learning," *Educational Leadership*, 63 (3), 10-17.

Van Horn, Royal (2007), "Van Horn's Rules," *Phi Delta Kappa*, 89 (3), 232-234.

2

CHAPTER

Teacher in School Setting

There are selected traits and characteristics which teachers need to possess. These need to be developed on a continuum. Growth needs to be continuous into achievement as a professional teacher. Possessing adequate subject matter knowledge is vital in teaching. This manuscript will emphasize personality factors which compliment academic knowledge.

Factors Necessary in a Quality Teacher

Feeling confident in one's ability to teach students from diverse cultures and achievement levels is important. Self-efficacy then is salient. This involves becoming proficient in being able to work well with students. Observing students in the classroom and noticing how they react to different styles of teaching assists in aiding learners to achieve more optimally. Here, the classroom teacher observes students in situations such as the following :

- individual endeavors as compared to learners working cooperatively.
- inductive versus deductive activities.

- activity centred as contrasted with subject matter experiences.
- a sound of purposeful busyness versus a quiet environment for learning.
- informal as compared to a formal seating arrangement (Searson and Dunn, 2001).

The teacher needs to reflect upon different strategies of teaching to notice under which conditions a given set of students do best. Learning then occurs on the teacher's part and, as a result, students may attain objectives more effectively. A new synthesis may accrue for the teacher in viewing previous with later approaches in teaching. Growth occurs with being better able to provide for individual differences in the classroom. Confidence comes about as a result of learning. Feelings of *self-efficacy* indicates increasing confidence in the self. This confidence is reflected within students who perceive the teacher as being able to reach different categories of learners in the classroom (Morgan and Williams, 2007).

Efficacious teachers tend to view the whole student in the evaluation process. There are definite needs which students individually possess. These must be met for learners to do well in school. Thus, pupils need to have adequate nutrition. They must possess energy to fulfil school tasks well. During the school year, most students receive breakfasts and the noon meal, if the latter possesses the needed money or not. There still are the evening meals and the weekends which are not accounted for. An increasing number of schools send home food packages for children to last during the weekend.

Clothing needs for the student must be met with properly fitting clothes as well as being appropriate for the season of the year. Schools here need to work with different charitable organizations. There are a plethora of homes which cannot provide for food and clothing needs of children. Unfortunate home situations abound where there is unemployment, as well as low wages and salaries for those employed. The kinds of shelters provided here may lack safety and/or adequate protection from the natural environment such as cold and hot weather, leaky roofs, among other disturbing factors. Contacting the proper authorities might provide some assistance in remediating difficulties. Dysfunctional families also hinder student achievement and progress in school. Thus, there are a plethora of hindrances which may keep students from doing well in school. Attempting to take care of the needs of students is a great chore with many involved difficulties (Woelfel, 2003).

Meeting psychological needs of learners is vital. Thus, pupils like to feel that they are a vital part of a group in the school/classroom setting. To be an isolate certainly does not take care of the necessity to belong. Feelings of belonging may be met in part by having pupils work in small groups on projects and activities. Membership in the group needs to be satisfying. Rude remarks, abrupt behavior, and negative criticisms hinder developing feelings of membership in a group. The pupils and his/her contributions need to be respected. The small group experience may include the following :

- construction of models related directly to the lesson/ unit being studied.
- problem solving involving indepth studies.
- creative art ideas pertaining to a major concept or generalization.
- dramatizing or pantomiming salient situations.
- oral activities in doing reports, participating in discussions, and debates, among others.
- peer teaching and peer interaction groups (Ediger, 2007).

The quality of human interaction is salient in these small group endeavors. Feelings of belonging might well come about if a caring environment is in the offing.

All like to have individual talents recognized. To never have attention given to what has been accomplished violates feelings of any student. If a learner achieves more than previously, this needs to be rewarded. Each pupil must attain as much as possible. Rewards in terms of genuine praise for accomplishments are musts. Esteem needs must be met (Covington, et.al., 2007).

When teaching pupils, the psychology of learning must be stressed, continuously. Thus, the pupil needs to experience fascinating learning activities. These activities engage learners in ongoing tasks. The interest factor shows up in pupil behavior resulting in eagerness to learn more. In addition to interest, pupils need to feel that relevancy is inherent in the ongoing activity. What is relevant is important to learn in ongoing lessons and units of study. The pupil then perceives significance in the curriculum. The learnings obtained are useful and may be used in school and in society. Motivation to learn increases with interest and purpose. A higher energy level for learning results. Meaning needs to be attached to acquired facts, concepts, and generalizations. When ideas are used, they become increasingly more meaningful. Learners modify meanings as they become functional. Feedback is secured from their use. The feedback provides direction for needed changes which must be made in teaching and learning. To truly comprehend, ideas, there needs to be meaning in each step of learning (Shepared, 2007).

Metacognition and the Teacher

Using the concept of metacognition helps to improve the quality of teaching as well as assisting pupils to progress. The teacher then engages in thinking about thinking. If the teacher has taught pupils, for example, how to solve a problem, he/she thinks back to how this was done sequentially. The teacher reflects upon questions such as the following:

- how were readiness experiences organized and presented?

- did I secure the attention of pupils with challenging and inspirational learning activities?
- did pupils ask on task questions relevant in problem solving?
- was information secured to answer questions effectively?
- were pupils able to perceive sequence in the problem solving activity?
- how did pupils assess progress in the problem solving approach?

By reviewing and analyzing previous learning activities, the teacher cognitively asks personal questions about teaching. The teacher then comes up with a new synthesis. Metacognition strategies assist the teacher to improve instruction by evaluating past experiences. Mentally, the teacher thinks about the previous and harmonizes that with new ideas in the thinking process. Workshops need to be conducted on metacognition applications in the school curriculum (Chamundeswari and Franky, 2008).

Related to metacognition is *monitoring* one's own teaching. Monitoring, for example, emphasizes if pupils are achieving rather than the teacher going through the motions of conducting a lesson. Thus, a pupil when reading aloud may be asked to say orally what was gleaned in terms of ideas read. If, he/she is a word caller largely, but does not comprehend content, the chances are the monitoring concept is not being emphasized. The purpose of reading is to comprehend facts, concepts, and generalizations. The teacher must monitor if pupils are truly achieving and not merely give the appearance of doing so. Pupils then, need to monitor the self to notice if comprehension is occurring and not merely reading words. Life in school and in society demands that the individual monitor what is being done to notice results. Strategies of learning may be changed if the results are not satisfactory, such as not comprehending subject matter while reading. Teachers must observe pupil progress carefully to notice if reading comprehension is being stressed (Ediger, 2007a&b).

A problem which exists in teaching pertains to pupils failing to experience quality sequence in learning. The Zone of Proximal Development (ZPD) is salient for teacher use. The ZPD emphasizes the difference between where the pupil is achieving presently as compared with a desired ideal. This zone may be minimized/eliminated through learning experiences provided by the teacher. Subsequent activities, carefully chosen and provided by the teacher, assist the pupil to achieve the desired objective. The ZPD concept must be kept in mind by the teacher to optimize learner achievement and progress. The teacher needs to have excellent knowledge of teaching and learning processes to minimize gaps in knowledge. These gaps must be reasonable and capable of being fulfilled with quality instruction (Vygotsky, 1978).

References

Chamundesweri, S., and Deepa Franky (2009), "Adjustment Patterns and Academic Achievement Among Students at the Secondary Level," *Meston Journal of Research in Education*, 7 (1), 12-21.

Covington, Lesa, *et al.* (2007), "Attitude Adjustments," *Educational Leadership*, 72-77.

Ediger, Marlow (2007a), "Meaning in Reading Instruction," *Reading Improvement*, 44 (4), 217-220.

Ediger, Marlow (2007b), "Teacher Observation to Assess Student Achievement," *Journal of Instructional Psychology*, 34 (3), 137-139.

Morgan, Denise N., and Jeffery L. Williams (2007), "Chapter Glancing: Noticing and Naming Chapter Openings," *The Reading Teacher*, 61 (2), 168-174.

Searson, Robert, and Rita Dunn (2001), "The Learning Styles Teaching Model," *Science and Children*, 38 (5) 22-27.

Shepared, Cynthia, et. al. (2007), "Inspiring Students to Create the Future," *Phi Delta Kappan*, 89 (3), 200-203.

Vygotsky, L. S. (1934/1978), *Mind and Society: The Development of Higher Psychological Processes*, Cambridge, Massachusetts: Harvard University Press.

Woelfel, Kay D, (2003), "Learner Centered Education" Implementing the Conceptual Framework-Moving from Theory to Action," *Education*, 124 (1), 17-23.

3 CHAPTER

Leadership in School Setting

It takes strong leaders to bring about positive changes in the elementary, middles schools, and high schools. Leaders are able to engage others in improving objectives of study, learning opportunities to achieve the stated objectives, as well as evaluation procedures. Designated leaders are the superintendent of schools, principals, curriculum directors, and department chairpersons, among others. Their roles are generally well-defined in terms of duties and responsibilities in respective leadership roles.

But what is the role of classroom teachers in providing leadership in improving the curriculum?

Teachers as Leaders

The classroom teacher may provide innumerable leadership roles in working toward improved teaching and learning situations. He/she makes many decisions in every day classroom procedures. How should pupils be grouped for instruction? There can be the class as a whole, small groups/ committees, and individualized study. When to use which procedure depends upon what assists pupils to achieve most optimally. Then too, there may be homogenous and heterogeneous plans of grouping for instruction. There are a plethora of additional decisions to be made such as the length of time devoted to each procedure as well as the sequence in individual learning activities (Ediger, 2007).

There are many contributions, teachers may make toward the larger picture of curriculum improvement. A teacher or team may volunteer to assist in inservice education programme. Thus, a plan may be developed and approved pertaining to improving reading instruction. Objectives of the inservice education programme might well include the role of phonics in providing for individual differences among learners. There are numerous issues in teaching phonics such as assisting learners as the need arises in an ongoing reading experiences as compared to teaching phonics prior to its actual use. Also, the intensity of phonics teaching needs clarification. Might sequential phonic learnings be developed within a complete unit of study in reading instruction? How should the use of context clues to ascertain unknown words be emphasized? Opposite of using these word recognition techniques in teaching reading is the Big Book approach. Beginning instruction, here, stresses holism in reading content together by pupils with teacher guidance. This is followed by pupils reading content individually (Landsman and Gorski, 40-44).

What then should be the role of phonics instruction in providing for individual differences among pupils in learning to read? Which parts of each of the following plans for teaching reading may be used to exemplify a quality programme of reading instruction?

- a basal reading programme with accompanying manual
- individualized reading using library books
- programmed reading with computer use
- reciprocal reading as well as questioning the author (QtA)
- Success for All (developed by Robert Siavin)
- scripted reading such as the Open Court series.

With the above named plans, teacher(s) conducting an inservice programme need to assist participants to analyze each programme. Brain storming may be one approach to use here. Conclusions need to be developed in reaching consensus from the brain storming activity as to which ingredients to use in coming up with the best procedure of reading instruction possible. An improved reading curriculum should result. Selected items from the brain storming experience might then be incorporated into the present program of instruction. If possible, it is good for the teacher to report back to the inservice participants how the change was perceived by pupils in the classroom (Ortlieb, *et al.*, 2007).

Issues in the Reading Curriculum

There are salient issues which teachers need to discuss. Sometimes, what was accepted as being "good" becomes an issue later. In the remediation arena, the following are considered as a basis for diagnosis and remedial teaching :

- a child repeating a word or phrase read correctly. This may be done by the reader to determine accuracy of what was read.
- looking back at what was read correctly. This might be done to check it the oral reading was done correctly.
- reading a word or phrase haltingly. This may occur when the reader is reading in a reflective manner.

Each of the above must be evaluated by the teacher to ascertain if fluency in reading is lacking or if there is an involved purpose in clarifying a purpose. When pupils substitute words for those in actual print, the teacher needs to notice if this distorts the meaning of the sentence, it may not be a serious error if sentence meaning remains intact. Otherwise, a more careful approach to word recognition must be stressed. These approaches may include the use of context clues, phonics, and syllabication analyses. Looking back at what was read might indicate the child is reflecting upon what was read to make certain of the accuracy of content read. In all cases, it is important to read as fluently as possible (Gammiil, 2006).

For inservice eduction, teacher leadership might well be involved in discussing the following :

- What is meant by fluency in reading?
- Should decoding skills be taught prior to a reading activity, or should they be taught as the need arises?
- What role does reflective thinking play in reading?
- How might pupils best reveal comprehension of what was read?
- How much emphasis should be placed upon peer learning in order to assist pupils in word recognition as well as in higher order of thinking skills?

A Professional Library for Teachers

Teachers may show leadership skills by assisting in establishing a professional library. A good approach in inservice education which is ongoing is for teachers to work cooperatively in developing a professional library for teachers. The professional library may be used within an inservice education program or separately as teachers have time to read professional literature in the teaching of reading. During school time or at home, reading the professional books should have as an objective for teachers to improve reading instruction. Professional textbooks in the teacher's library should contain content in the following areas of instruction :

- diverse work recognition/decoding skills
- whole language experiences for children
- an integrated curriculum
- different plans in teaching reading
- means of assessing/evaluating learner achievement and progress

- organizing the reading curriculum
- innovations in reading instruction
- developing wholesome attitudes
- developmental programs in teaching and learning
- creative approaches in teaching reading.

Professional books in the teaching of reading may be obtained. There are several periodicals, as a minimum, which should also be an inherent part of a professional library for teachers.

Teachers must have time to analyze and discuss literature pertaining to the teaching of reading. Critical and creative thinking as well as problem-solving need to be involved. Making use of ideas read and sharing these with colleagues is important in inservice education (Ediger, 2003).

Developing Grade Level Meetings

As a university supervisor of student teachers, the writer spoke with the principal of a participating school who stated that grade level meetings begun two years ago had truly stimulated improved instruction.

The teachers established goals, meeting dates, and kept a running account of what transpired.

A team of teachers might then work with others on the same grade level or in a combination of grades such as the primary or intermediate grades. The mechanics and logistics for each meeting should be cooperatively determined. Within these meetings, problems in teaching should be discussed such as the following :

- developing and maintaining pupil interest among special needs children
- motivating learners to achieve
- establishing purpose for learning
- helping struggling readers

- assisting English Language Learners (ELL)
- teaching pupils to attain mandated objectives
- seeking a commercial reading program to help learners progress (Ediger and Rao, 2007).

Minutes of each meeting should be kept and distributed among school personnel. Sharing of ideas among grade levels is important. They might well be tried out in different classrooms with feed back provided to the involved group. Methods of inservice education should be a motivating factor to improve reading instruction!

REFERENCES

Ediger, Marlow (2003), "Data driven decision making," *College Student Journal*, 37(1), 9-15.

Ediger, Marlow (2007), "Teacher observation to assess learner achievement,", *Journal of Instructional Psychology,"* 34(3), 137-1 39.

Ediger, Marlow, and D. Bhaskara Rao (2007), *Reading curriculum and instruction*. New Delhi, India: Discovery publishing house.

Landsman, Julie, and Paul Gorski (2007), Countering standardization," *Educational Leadership*, 64 (8), 40-44.

Gammill, Deidra M. (2006), "Learning the write way," *The Reading Teacher*, 59 (8), 754- 763.

Ortlieb, Evan, *et al.* (2007),The art of reading; dramatizing literacy," *Reading improvement*, 44 (3), 169-176.

4

CHAPTER

Student Mobility and Learning

Many students move from one school district to the next. Perhaps, this occurs several times in one school year. When moving from city to city or state to state, there are feelings experienced by these involved children. Old friends and teachers are left behind, new ones need to be made. Different kinds of school buildings and grounds are experienced during these changing times. The school curriculum may be quite different as compared to that of the sending school. Thus, the level of complexity and subject matter content in the objectives may differ much from the school previously attended. What are selected steps to take to welcome the new student into the school setting?

Welcoming the New Student

As soon as possible, the receiving school needs to secure information from the former school on items such as the following, among others :

- the age and grade level of the student as well as the names of the parents or custodians and their level of education

- where the student is in achievement in the different areas of the school curriculum. Which specific modifications, if any, are made for the student?
- which specific units of study the student is presently engaged in. Sequence in learning is important in harmonizing what was studied in the sending school as compared to the ensuing course of study in the receiving school (Horejsi, 2003).

Information received must be used to inform the new teacher(s) and is to be used in determining how best to meet needs of the learner. The new teacher must be optimistic about receiving information from the sending school in that a student might react differently to the new teacher as compared to those of the past. Selected students respond differently to different teachers and may turn out as higher achievers as compared to what was indicated in the report from the receiving school.

Personal information such as hobbies and interests of new students may be obtained when occasions arise such as the student mentioning hobbies and interests in class discussions or when consulting with the teacher. It is good to use these when opportunities arise within the curriculum. This might be a motivator for the student.

When the new student arrives in school, he/she needs to be introduced to classmates. Prior to his/her arrival in school, classmates should experience readiness. Thus, the class needs to have knowledge of the arrival of a new student. The new student must develop immediate feelings of belonging and acceptance. A peer may be appointed to serve as a mentor to orientate the learner. Politeness and caring should be hall marks of these peers. Rudeness and impolite behavior should not be in evidence in the classroom or school setting (Ediger, 2006).

The new student should begin teaching and learning experiences with his/her present achievement level and then progress optimally in a sequential manner. Learning experiences should :

- develop and maintain student interests.
- stress goal centered behavior and engage the learner.
- emphasize new subject matter built upon previous learnings.
- assist in achieving major concepts and generalizations.
- help the student to perceive purpose in learning.
- guide the learner to relate subject matter acquired to. the self, to society, and to other related ideas having been studied.
- be useful and practical (See Brozo and Flynt).

Mobile students, in particular, must feel welcome and aided to make friends and develop feelings of belonging. They may have moved around to several schools as the father/mother has been transferred to different jobs. Jobs and positions may well lack security and the offspring moves along to a new location with his/her parents. A divorce may also make for separation of a family and a child is left in a situation where moving to a new location is definitely possible. Death or illness of a parent also may make moving a possibility. Whatever, the reason for moving to a different school, the school age child needs to experience as much security as possible. The transition must be made as smoothly as possible with much effort put forth to make it a reality (Petrus, 2006).

Working Cooperatively and Individually

The learning style of the transfer student must be provided for. He/she may prefer a combination of group and individual endeavors. In society, both are important in that people need to work cooperatively in a harmonious manner at the work place and home. Thus, cooperative learning needs to be emphasized. Here, students must learn to respect each others ideas and contributions. They attempt to harmonize ideas in a small group setting. Perseverance is important on engaged tasks so that goals are being achieved. A problem is identified and an hypothesis developed. Information from a variety of sources are used to secure necessary answers and to test the hypothesis. Relevant information is sorted from the irrelevant in problem solving. Critical thinking is used to separate the accurate from the inaccurate, the salient from that of lesser value, as well as fantasy from reality. Also, creative thinking is uses since novel solutions to problems may be necessary. The "tried and the true" may not work in problem solving situations. Much effort is needed to work well with others and to complete a problem solving activity (Ediger, 2007).

Committees at work in problem-solving situations is one way to assist the new student to develop feelings of belonging. Acceptance of each other and assisting where it is needed are salient in cooperative learning endeavors. Recognition needs of the student must be met in developing a good self concept. Success in engaged endeavors in problem solving as well as praise received for quality contributions made aid the learner to feel worthy, welcome, and appreciated. The feeling dimension of any person is important to consider for optimal achievement to take place (Ediger, 2008).

The new student needs to grow and progress in the following areas of human progress :

- social development. Working together well with others is important now as well as at the future work place.
- emotional development. Positive feelings toward the self and toward others aids the individual in achieving well in society.
- values in life. Values guide a person in making choices from among alternatives in every day living. They include honesty, decency, and fairness.
- wisdom. The wise person persists in making positive choices. The school curriculum must provide ample

opportunities for students to make choices in terms of objectives to achieve, learning activities to pursue, as well as means of evaluation of progress.

- knowledge objectives. They need to provide background information to perceive problems and solve problematic situations (Noddings, 2008).

Education should consist of both - quality and values for the overall development of the student and for the nation and benefit of society. While quality caters for head and hands, values cater to the heart. Few centuries ago education included both of these. As time passed, gradually values have been overlooked and finally dropped plunging humanity into chaos and danger. The remedy is to reinduct them. It is being endeavored at the highest level in this direction but half hearted implementation of measures would not only be useless but also a waste of time, money, and efforts. It is a matter of great satisfaction that there are several institutions wherein this sort of education is imparted. The step may be small but is significant and inspiring (Rao, 2008).

Reading and the Transfer Student

There is a considerable amount of reading that students do in the different curriculum areas. The present reading level. of the transfer student needs to be sought by the teacher. A student should be able to identify approximately ninety-five per cent of the running words read aloud correctly from a basal text. If the identified words run increasingly below the 95 per cent level, it will hinder comprehension of subject matter. One reads content to secure ideas and not for the sake of "reading" without comprehending. From the approximate ninety five percent level of correct word recognition selection, the student also needs to be able to answer three of four comprehension questions correctly covering the pursued content. This is an informal method of ascertaining if subject-matter read is on the understanding level of the transfer student.

There are methods of word recognition techniques to scaffold student learning in reading. The following techniques may be used :

- context clues whereby the learner is assisted in providing a word for the unknown which makes sense. Generally, the surrounding words of the unknown will provide clues. Sometimes, a student will give a ridiculous word for the unidentified. He/she may be guided to notice if that word makes sense in the total sentence, or even paragraph.
- phonics clues in which a student is assisted to look at the beginning consonant of the unknown word and then ascertain which word would be meaningful in relations to others in the sentence/paragraph. Beginning consonants together with context clues may be a meaningful approach in identifying unknown words (Ediger and Rao, 2007).

Quality sequence may be in the offing when higher levels of cognition are stressed in the comprehension of subject matter read. Thus, critical and creative thinking are salient to stress within the problem solving arena.

IN CONCLUSION

The transfer student needs assistance in becoming a member of the new classroom as well as in small group work. Developing feelings of belonging are important. The transfer student needs to feel welcome in the new surroundings. The learner also must have esteem needs met. He/she needs to feel that salient contributions can be made in the school and classroom setting. Sequential learnings aid the transfer student to achieve as optimally as possible within the framework of rich learning activities.

References

Brozo, William, and E. Sutton Flynt (2007), "Content Literacy: Fundamentals of Toolkit Elements," *The Reading Teacher*, 61 (2),192-197.

Ediger, Marlow (2006), "Administration of Schools," *College Student Journal*, 40 (4), 846-851.

Ediger, Marlow (2007), "Meaning in Reading Instruction," *Reading Improvement*, 44 (4). K217-220.

Ediger, Marlow (2008), Mental Health in the Curriculum," *Journal of Instructional Psychology*, 35 (1), 38-42.

Ediger, Marlow, and D. Bhaskara Rao (2007), *Reading Curriculum and Instruction*. New Delhi, India : Discovery Publishing House.

Horejsi, Martin (2003), "Making Technology Inclusive," *Science and Children*, 41 (3),20-24.

Noddings, Nel (2008), "All Our Students Thinking," *Educational Leadership*, 65 (5), 8-13.

Petrus, Ken (2006), "An Operational Definition of Class Participation/ *College Student Journal*, 40 (4), 821-823.

Rao, C. Shobha (2008), "Quality and Values: Obverse and Reverse of the Modern Education Coin," *Edutracks*, 7 (8), 20-22.

5

CHAPTER

Cooperative Learning and Pupil

Much writing in professional journals and speeches presented at teacher education conventions pertain to the importance of cooperative learning. Pupils are to share ideas as well as engage in small group work, rather than in individual endeavours. This philosophy of instruction is, in part, based on the writings of Vygotsky (1933-1978). Vygotsky believed that pupils learn best in social situations whereby ideas circulate among members in the group. As these ideas "bump off the minds" of participants, they are learned by members.

Learning in social situations may be compared with individual endeavors whereby each pupil works on assignments, tasks, and problem solving experiences by the self. To be sure, learning opportunities will not be cooperative nor individualistic continuously, but the emphasis will be on one as compared to the other, during a given school day (Ediger, 2007).

Advantages of Cooperative Learning

There are a plethora of reasons which may be given in emphasizing cooperative learning. The following, among others, are salient :

- decisions made in organizations, clubs, and councils, are made with within a membership. The larger unit may be quite formal with its strict hierarchical lines of organization or flexible when the informal group is quite small and there is less need for formality. Group interaction among its members include the following :
  * pupils, as well as adults, interact frequently in group settings. This may be true of informal conversations among participants.
  * individuals might well ask for assistance from a group when problems arise and help is necessary.
  * feelings of security may be found in a small group setting.
  * pupils like to feel they belong in a group.
  * individuals are social beings and like to affiliate with others (Maslow 1954).

Problem-solving methods tend to stress small group endeavors in the classroom setting. Here, pupils with teacher assistance identify a problem area in an ongoing unit of study. The problem involves deliberation and thinking is stressed. Thus in a social studies unit of study, pupils may identify the following :

- Why did the Ottoman Empire collapse at the end of World War One?
- Why did Great Britain receive mandates to rule Palestine, Iraq, and Jordan whereas France mandated Syria and Lebanon following World War I ?
- What was the significance of the Balfour Declaration of 1917 as well as the MacMahon-Hussein correspondence of 1915?
- How did each of the Mandates affect the Middle East? (Ediger, 1997).

Problems chosen need to be developmentally appropriate. Four to five classmates should be on each committee of their very own choosing. Reference materials need to be discussed and readily available. Encyclopaedias, library books, resource personnel who have lived in the Middle East, video tapes, and especially the computer and the internet are valuable sources of information in gathering information to assist in solving the above asterisked problems.

The teacher needs to be certain that pupils understand flexible rules for engaging in committee work; these include the following :

- each member needs to participate.
- no one should dominate committee procedures.
- participants need to communicate ideas clearly.
- questions should be asked if a contribution is not understood or if a new problem arises.
- courtesy toward and consideration for others are two concepts to emphasize in small group endeavors.
- the teacher is a consultant, not a lecturer nor bystander.
- the committee is to work for the good of the group (Parker, 2001).

If more than one committee is in operation, then progress reports may be made to other committees. An atmosphere of encouragement to do good work must prevail. Summaries of committee endeavors may also be made to the total class. These can be made in chart form and posted on a nearby wall. If a project is involved, the completed construction item, too, needs to be displayed so that classmates and pupils from other classrooms may observe and ask questions about each. The completed work might well be assessed in terms of the following criteria :

- accuracy stressed in the total activity,
- active participation by each committee member,
- neatness in ongoing experiences,

- appreciation for committee work,
- positive attitudes toward others.

Problem-solving and project methods might well lend themselves to additional cooperative activities in ensuing lessons and units of study. Pupil interests and purposes should be inherent in each identified problem and project. It is the pupil that needs to do the learning and the teacher needs to supervise the ongoing experiences and informally evaluate progress to determine if learners achieved objectives of instruction.

It is important that each member participates fully in cooperative learning. The writer's daughter did not appreciate cooperative learning as a junior high school student when working as a member of the yearbook committee. She felt alone in doing most of the work while the other members were content to be observers. The teacher must observe that all participate in completing an activity. Members work together to fulfill plans in problem solving or in completing a project (Bembemutty, 2008).

Pupils Individually Achieving Objectives

Somewhat opposite in grouping pupils for instruction is to assist learners to work individually on an activity. There are educators who state that individual preferences versus cooperative learning pertain to learning styles and not that one is superior to the other. Perhaps, both are salient in that life itself emphasizes interaction with others as well as being able to do things by the self. Sometimes, the two are inseparable. There are a plethora of experiences which are highly profitable for individual endeavours. These include the following :

- reading activities in ongoing units of study or for sheer enjoyment
- writing experiences in different curriculum areas as in narrative, expository, and creative endeavors

- viewing and listening to content from a video tape
- practicing an oral report to be given in class
- doing a drawing to summarize acquired learnings from a reading/listening activity
- inventing and playing a game (Noddings, 2008).

With individual work, the pupil needs adequate background information to participate in achieving an objective. He/she must monitor the self to notice if progress is being made. Self reflection is salient in reviewing what has been learned, what is left to learn, and additional learnings desired. It is significant for the learner to become efficacious, thus becoming increasingly confident with ample needed knowledge, skills, and appropriate attitudes. Many of these behaviours are equally salient in cooperative learning.

With individual tasks, the teacher may carefully monitor leaner progress, for example, in specific learnings such as the following :

- answering questions from a basal textbook covering subject matter read,
- doing a bulletin board display,
- pantomiming a scene from a library book,
- writing specific kinds of poetry in an English assignment,
- drawing a map showing historic location of a place,
- completing a mathematics assignment involving addition of fractions,
- setting up a science experiment (Sharma and Sharma, 2009).

There are a plethora of individual learning experiences for pupils. Each of the above asterisked activities might also be done in a cooperative setting. The point is that pupils should achieve as optimally as possible, be it in individual or in cooperative endeavors.

Criteria to utilize in evaluating pupils on individual tasks performed include the following :

- perceived effort put forth in learning
- quality of meticulous work in ongoing experiences
- revealing an attitude of desiring to do well in assignments as well as in voluntary endeavors
- use of leisure time in a profitable way
- self evaluation of ongoing as well as of completed school work
- reflection of what has been learned and identification of what is left to learn
- a desire to learn in school and in society (Phillips *et al.* 2008).

Balance in the Curriculum

The teacher needs to seek balance between cooperative learning and individual endeavors. Both procedures are highly worthwhile if they :

- assist in providing for optimal learner progress
- engage pupils in learning
- secure and maintain learner interests
- help pupils to feel that achieving stated objectives is indeed worthwhile
- guide pupils to perceive sequence in learning
- provide for learning styles of pupils
- emphasize relevance in the curriculum (Ediger, 2009).

IN CLOSING

A variety of learning opportunities must be used to promote individual and social development of pupils. In addition to those alluded to previously, ample experiences need to be provided in the use of technology and computers in the achievement of objectives of instruction. Thus, pupils might well work on programs individually as well as in cooperative learning. Computerized programmes need to be stimulating, challenging, and developmental appropriate.

References

Bembemutty, Heifer (2009), "Feeling-of-Knowing Judgment and Self Regulation of Learning," *Education*, 129 (4), 589-598.

Ediger, Marlow (1997), *The Holy Land.* Kirksville, Missouri: Simpson Publishing Company.

Ediger, Marlow (2007), *Language Arts Education.* New Delhi, India: Discovery Publishing House.

Ediger, Marlow (2008), "Psychology of Parental Involvement in Reading," *Reading Improvement,* 45 (1), 46-52.

Ediger, Marlow (2009), "Technical Education, the Work Place, and the Student," *ATEA Journal*, 36 (2), 18-19.

Maslow, Abraham (1954), *Motivation and Personality.* New York: Harper and Row.

Noddings, Nel (2008), "All Our Students Thinking," *Educational Leadership*, 65(5), 9-13.

Parker, Walter C. (2001), *Social Studies in Elementary Education.* Columbus, Ohio : Prentice-Hall, Inc., Chapter Eleven.

Phillips, Antionette S. *et al.* 2008), "Enhancing A Curriculum: A Focus on the Developmental Process," *College Student Journal*, 42 (4),1070-1074.

Sharma, Mala, and Sumar Sharma (2009), "Attitude of Science Teachers Towards the Project Method," *Edutracks*, 8 (6), 40-43. Printed in India.

Vygotsky, Lin (1933-1978), *Mind in Society. Cambridge*, Massachusetts: Harvard University Press.

6

CHAPTER

Teaching and Learning is more than Setting Standards

The setting of standards for pupils to achieve has become a national past time in education. State standards and national standards have become salient topics for writing as well as for speaking at national education conferences. It almost appears that the only important concept pertaining to teaching is standards. The standards movement has its initial beginnings in behaviorism as a psychology of learning. E. L. Thorndike (1874-1946) advocated that "whatever exists, exists in some amount, and if it exists in some amount, it can be measured". Tests were then developed as time went on in mathematics, reading, science, social studies, and spelling, among others, to measure achievement in these academic/ curriculum areas.

Generally, multiple choice test items are written by selected educators and policy-makers to measure achievement. Test results then can be evaluated rather quickly with printouts, from computers, which tell how well a pupil, school, and/or school system is performing numerically. Precision is involved such as a pupil ranking on the fiftieth percentile, for example, meaning that for every 100 pupils tested, fifty are above and fifty below the fiftieth percentile. With machine scoring, mass numbers of tests may be scored in a relatively short period of time.

Standardization of Tests

Measurement of pupil achievement has usually gone in the direction of standardized test use. Standardized tests emphasize the following :

- the directions for test taking are clearly written and are the same for all pupils taking the test,
- the time limits for test taking are the same for all,
- the scoring key is the same for all pupils taking the test on a particular grade level,
- raw scores of pupils from test taking then are compared with those of the norm group in the Manual. This provides percentiles, stanines, grade equivalent, and/or age equivalent ranks. Percentiles are generally used and tend to be the easiest to understand.

Orderliness and specificity are key concepts in measurement philosophy of evaluation. Standardized test results emphasize comparing one pupil with another and one school/school system with another. Comparisons in achievement might well also involve comparisons among states and nations.

Goals in making these comparisons are numerous such as :

- eliminating achievement gaps between and among different minority/majority groups of pupils,
- providing a standard for grade promotion,
- identifying weak schools and working toward a "turn around",
- permitting pupils to attend satisfactory schools which have met appropriate standards,
- free tutoring given to failing pupils,
- topping the list among nations of the world in academic achievement with international tests.

There are a plethora of criticisms in using measurement philosophy in determining achievement of pupils which includes the following :

- only what can be measured in achievement become test items on tests. Thus, factual test items accrue. This leaves out many important facets of accomplishment such as being a good citizen, having empathy toward others, and treating others with respect. Attempts made in testing on the last three concepts have made for low reliability in test results.
- omission of selected curriculum areas in testing due to a focus on the basics of reading and mathematics. Science may be added also, but social studies, the fine arts, and physical education are omitted as in No Child Left Behind (NCLB).
- unreasonable standards to achieve for English Language Learners (ELL), special needs learners, and slow learners. These pupils must meet the same standards as do other levels of pupil achievement such as the gifted and the talented.
- time limits for test taking being the same for all. There are pupils who need more time to answer questions on tests as compared to others due to individual differences.
- multiple choice test items used in testing. Factual knowledge is easiest to test upon. These limit pupils in evaluating thinking abilities. Critical thinking and problem solving are very salient in school and in society.
- omission of any reference to determining achievement in *discussions*. In school and in society, much emphasis is placed upon discussions to assist in analyzing and synthesizing ideas.
- high stakes testing involved. With high stakes testing, one test determines promotion of pupils to the next

grade level in NCLB. This is an inadequate system of evaluation. More sources of information should be used here in addition to high stakes test scores. There are too many reasons why a test score was low for a pupil on the day of testing such as ill-health, tenseness about home ituations, and emotional upsets.

Further questions and problems arise when viewing test items themselves. Too frequently, people feel that a test score is an absolute. However, tests are developed by human beings and they attempt to measure what is felt to be salient. There are problems in writing test items such as are they truly valid? Not all schools will have stressed the same objectives and thus there are learners who have not experienced that which is covered in a standardized test. Test items, too, in selected cases may not have been written with clarity, even if upmost care is taken in their writing. Computer glitches have caused heart ache for selected parents who received noticed their offspring had failed only to find out later that a glitch in scoring was involved. Mass numbers of tests are scored each school year with the accountability movement in vogue.

Teachers have drilled students on test taking before a standardize test is given such as the NCLB. Drill amounts to memorization and educational psychologists frown upon drill as a major method of teaching. It is more important for pupils to understand and attach meaning to what is taught. Learners, also, need to perceive purpose in learning. It would be difficult for a pupil to perceive purpose in endless amount of drill, merely to do well on a test. Testing is not an authentic task; people in society do not show their talents and abilities through testing, but by actually performing work in a life like situation. Certainly, a correlational study should be made of how test scores on standardized tests relate to success at the work place. Do tests truly measure what is salient to know and do in order to succeed in society?

Adequate yearly progress (AYP) has been almost impossible to achieve in No Child Left Behind. Schools are almost destined to fail with AYP goals to be met by 2014.

Generally, Manuals are developed to assist pupils in studying for taking a standardized test. It would be important to know if there is a level playing field in that all have access to the same/similar kind of tutoring, prior to test taking. What about including family income levels, nutrition, safety, and a rich home/community learning environment? The profit motive is involved in developing tests and accompanying Manuals. The profit motive should not over take attempts to ascertain how well pupils are truly achieving (Ediger, 2001).

Constructivism in Teaching

Constructivism as a psychology/philosophy of instruction does not place major emphasis upon stating objectives prior to instruction. However, there are general guidelines in which direction instruction will be taking place. Instead of determining objectives, prior to instruction, the teacher guides learners to attach meaning to and sequence learning experiences. It is the learner who will sequence or order experiences; the teacher encourages and assists pupils in achievement. The focal point of instruction is upon the pupil. Each pupil possesses unique differences from others. The teacher needs to understand the background of each learner in order to understand previous experiences of pupils. Responsibility for learning resides within each pupil. Motivation for learning differs from child to child, and the teacher needs to properly motivate pupils in the classroom. If a pupil does not understand a concept or generalization, the teacher raises questions for which the learner thinks about answers, which in sequence lead to understanding and meaning. He/she does not lecture ready made knowledge and skills for pupil digestion, but rather helps learners to find their own information.

Problem-solving emphasizes constructivism in teaching and learning. Here, pupils in an authentic setting identify a relevant problem for which solutions need to be sought. The problem possesses relevance and requires diligence as well as effort in working toward a solution. An hypothesis is developed and tested with vital information gathered from a variety of sources. The hypothesis is then accepted, modified, or rejected. New problems may arise in the ongoing experience for which solutions are needed.

Project methods also stress elements of constructivism in that a concrete product is ultimately produced. Thus, a purpose for the project is envisioned by learners. The purpose, for example, is to develop a model or object, directly arising from interests developed within the unit of study being pursued. Specific plans are made for the construction activity which are then carried out and results in the final product. Evaluation standards need to be crafted to appraise the product.

Committee endeavours are involved in doing projects as well as for problem solving. Cooperatively developed standards for each experience is salient. In each activity, pupils are heavily involved in sequencing their very own learnings. Interest in the experience provides effort and motivation for learning. Pupils are actively involved in ongoing learning experiences and this is an ideal emphasized by constructivists.

There is considerable interaction among pupils in committee endeavours, based on their interests. Pupils are heavily involved in ordering and perceiving sequence in tasks pursued. They assist in determining objectives, learning activities, integrating subject matter, as well as appraising achievement. The teacher has important responsibilities in being a guide, a helper, and one who is able to motivate and encourage learners in ongoing experiences. Pupils generate knowledge and skills from past and ongoing experiences. Teachers do not impart knowledge and skills, but rather assist pupils to make discoveries inductively.

IN SUMMARY

Two somewhat opposing schools of thought were emphasized in teaching and learning situations. Measurement theory stresses the use of testing to evaluate achievement pupil achievement. Here, multiple choice test items are used to ascertain learner progress in learning. Data from test results are highly precise and presented in numerical terms. The objectives for the test are predetermined and available for teachers as guidelines to use in teaching. Specific levels of accomplishment for each learner need to be met in order to be promoted to the next grade level or to exit from high school. Teaching toward pupils achieving precise objectives is salient.

Toward the other end of the continuum, constructivism is quite open ended and leaves pupil leeway in the selection of objectives, learning opportunities, and evaluation procedures. The teacher is a guide and motivator of pupil achievement. Learning by discovery is a key component in instruction.

References

Ediger, Marlow (2002), *Psychology and the Curriculum.* New Delhi, India: Discovery Publishing House.

7

CHAPTER

How Specific Should Objectives be Written?

The degree of specificity of objectives is certainly an issue. How specific then should objectives of instruction be written? Generally, it is considered that objectives need to be written in measurable terms. Thus, the teacher can measure, after instruction, if a pupil has/has not achieved an objective. The emphasis then is placed upon measuring achievement. It must be measured if a learner has been successful in learning. The quality of objectives, too frequently, has been if they are precise enough for measurement to occur, then they are well stated. Which weaknesses then are in evidence?

Measurably stated Objectives and the Pupil

Might all important subject matter for pupil achievement be written in measurable terms? This has been a frequent problem. Tests are written to measure what is stated in the objective for pupil achievement. Thus, subject matter and processes for learner attainment must be written in specific terms. Usually, multiple choice test items are used to ascertain pupil achievement. Some objectives are indeed complex, if not impossible, to state measurably. Can the following be stated in measurable terms?

- being a caring person
- acting responsibly in life
- treating others with respect
- liking a curriculum area
- enjoyment in reading for recreational reasons
- performing science experiments and demonstrations (Ediger and Rao, 2001).

Measurably stated mandated objectives generally dominate all other kinds of objectives for pupil attainment. There is no leeway then for pupil's identification of problems areas, working on projects, as well as pursuing a special worthwhile interest. Measurably stated objectives are stated prior to instruction and leave no room for questions from learners. Then too, pupils are tested on what is mandated for teaching and what is mandated is the focal point of testing. The rest, what is not tested, has little or no worth. Reading, mathematics, and science are three academic areas in which pupils are tested annually. This leaves out social studies and the fine arts. Schools are to look good on test results. Thus, if only reading, mathematics, and science, achievement are tested, these three curriculum areas will receive major/sole attention, in many cases. A narrowing of the curriculum occurs. The other curriculum areas are ignored or minimized (Ediger, 2003).

Learning activities are to be aligned with the mandated objectives. Are there other learning activities which are important for the *learner* to experience which are not aligned with the stated objectives? Do the aligned learning activities, too, narrow the curriculum further? If what is tested, will be what is taught, then the answer would have to be "Yes." If test results are all that matter, then only what is on the test should be taught. This assumes that the stated objectives which go along with the test are available to classroom teachers. Otherwise when drill is stressed for test taking, teachers guess what subject-matter might be included thereon.

From the viewpoint of educational psychologists, drill is still frowned upon as a method of teaching (Noddings, 2008).

There is more to education than passing tests on subject-matter knowledge which is measurable on standardized tests and machine scored. The feelings, attitudes, values, and personal interests are also important, but not measured. Also, it is difficult to determine what is valuable for pupils to achieve in subject matter. Human beings write test items and are these absolutes? What might the correlation be between high test scores and success in life (Adams and Pierce, 2003)?

Many writers of educational articles in journals say that teachers should focus on the academics. What value is this for individuals who will be working in the non-academic areas of life in the future work place? Good carpenters, brick layers, carpet installers, plumbers, and health technicians, among others,will always be important. Do pupils turn off on schooling when their unique interests are minimized? Teach for the standard tests has become a slogan. This emphasizes drill, which educational psychologists have long frowned upon as a method of teaching. Instead methods of teaching need to be varied to provide for individual differences. For secondary pupils, technical education should be in the offing as choices for learners.

Standardized tests stress that :

- all pupils regardless of ability level take the same test for those on the same grade level. No provision is made for those who are talented or of lesser ability levels.
- the time limits for test taking are the same for all. There is no provision made for pupils who differ from each other in the amount of time needed to take a standardized time.
- machines are used to score tests. Multiple choice test items are used with no input into interpretation or involved creativity in student responses.

- subject matter used in tests is take out of context. Relationships to ongoing units of studies and lessons are not emphasized (Ediger, 2005).

There might well be other/additional methods in the evaluation of pupil achievement including portfolios, teacher observations and related recordings made, teacher written tests including essay test items, and pupil self evaluation in terms of criteria.

Effect Upon Pupils in Taking Mandated Tests

Mandated testing requires levels of pupil proficiency in order to be promoted to the next grade level, such as passing tests in grades three through eight and once on the secondary school level. Failure is truly a defeating experience. The self concept is lowered when individual pupils experience a major failure. If enough pupils fail a test, then there are a plethora of learners held back which might cause a problem in classroom space. When recommendations are made by diverse high profile individuals and groups, they generally advocate more demanding subject-matter for pupils to encounter in classes. "Higher expectations from pupils are necessary to optimize pupil achievement," becomes a slogan. Critics of public school pupil achievement also emphasize more pupils take Algebra 2, in the school curriculum. Content should not be dubbed down.

The answer to these critics involve the following :

- learning should be meaningful and pupils need to understand what is taught. Subject-matter not understood by pupils makes for more failure in classes taken. Why? If the teacher moves on to ensuing learnings for pupils, it will be difficult to understand the new with a lack of background experiences.
- interest is important in learning. The learner and the subject-matter become one and not separate entities.

When "all" need to take certain classes, then there is much forcing of pupils to achieve what is not of interest. Lower levels of subject-matter is then taught and emphasized due to the present achievement levels of selected pupils in a class.

- purpose is salient. In learning pupils needs to perceive reasons for engaging in an ongoing lesson or unit of study (See Guilfoyle, 2006).

Somewhat opposite of measurably stated objectives psychology is constructivism. Constructivism stresses the importance of the learner being actively involved in decision making in the curriculum. Thus, the pupil has input into decisions which affect him/her in classwork. To have decisions for mandated objectives and evaluation procedures come from on high might be quite far removed from the pupil's own understanding, interests, and purposes. In fact, with measurably stated objectives, the pupil is completely left out of making choices as to what and how to learn. His/her own questions and concerns do count in constructivist psychology. From among alternatives, the pupil's choice of reading materials, problems to solve, projects to do, and assessment procedures are planned cooperatively with the involved learner (See Umesh, 2007).

References

Adams, Cheryll, and Rebecca I. Pierce (2003), "Teaching by Tiering," *Science and Children*, 41 (3), 30-34.

Ediger, Marlow (2003), "Data Driven Decision Making," *College Student Journal*, 37 (1), 9-15.

Ediger, Marlow (2005), "Themes to Emphasize in the Geography Curriculum," *Journal of Instructional Psychology*, 32 (2), 160-163.

Ediger, Marlow, and D. Bhaskara Rao (2001), *Teaching Social Studies Successfully*. New Delhi, India: Discovery Publishing House.

Guilfoyle, Christy (2006), "NCLB: Is There Life Beyond Testing," *Educational Leadership*, 64 (3), 8-13.

Noddings, Nel (2008), "All Our Students Thinking," *Educational Leadership*, 65 (5), 8-13.

Umesh, Dr. (2007), "Assuring Quality of Teacher Education in Present Scenario," *Edutracks*, 6 (9), 13-15.

8 CHAPTER

Disagreements with Selected Educational Goals

Why all the emphasis upon what *selected* educators and policy makers recommend? There are salient ideas in education which are advocated continuously. It almost sounds like a stuck record. There needs to be adequate debate and discussion among public school personnel, professors of education, educational philosophers and psychologists to agree upon what should be emphasized in the curriculum. Educators must definitely have their voices expressed in a rational discussion, not like some town meetings we have heard on television during the presidential campaign. Nor should these meetings emphasize opinions as are given in a TV newscast whereby those with opposite beliefs shout at each other, refusing to hear what the opposition says. Nothing is accomplished with rudeness, intimidation, making damaging remarks, and setting the stage for dissension. Rather, civility should prevail in which quality listening occurs among knowledgeable persons. Quality background information should be at the finger tips of participants. The moderator in debates needs to be as unbiased as possible and enforce established rules. He/she must be a good listener and contribute expertise, not shoddy dogmatic statements which cannot be substantiated with critical thinking. A shouting match does not accomplish anything but hostility and anger. Merely trying to confuse the other participants with "holier than thou" remarks is defeating. Rather, carefully construed ideas based on an adequate knowledge base, as well as theory, should prevail.

Participants must be informed individuals on issues being discussed. Decisions need to be based on the psychology of learning and how it affects pupils in teaching and learning situations, not on haughtiness, aloofness, and the profit motive. Dogmatic thinking must be avoided.

Setting Standards

When listening to many policy-makers, the thinking is that education *consists* of standards set in advance for pupil achievement. The standards movement stresses that the basics identified by policy makers must be achieved by all pupils. This eliminates the factor that learners differ from each other in a multiplicity of ways such as interest, motivation, purpose, and abilities. Why all the emphasis placed upon standards? Could it be that regardless of status of standards achievement by pupils, it is not adequate and needs to be lambasted by higher ups who are divorced from teaching? What justification is there for pupils acquiring the knowledge and skills in these standards? It appears that pupils and teachers thinking does not matter in selecting objectives. The writer wonders what correlation would there be between pupils doing well on the tests and future success at the work place or happiness in life.

Too frequently, standards, such as No Child Left Behind (NCLB) represents punishment if pupils do not attain what is deemed necessary, such as not being promoted from one grade level to the next. If pupils fail, the self-concept goes downhill. It may be justified to have some kind of criteria to govern "what should be in education," but these need to be

- voluntary to notice how well pupils "measure up" to selected criteria

- used as one standard, among others, in promotion of pupils
- stressed as objectives for pupils to achieve with others, as determined by teachers and pupils, as well as school principals
- flexible so that meaningful learning opportunities may be chosen, involving pupil/teacher input
- written so that teaching to a test is not recommendable or possible.

Test results do not necessarily determine how well a pupils will do in life. Outside of formal education, individuals do not take tests to reveal how well an individual performs at a work place. It is the quality deeds and acts that matter. Testing is one method to ascertain how well a pupil is achieving, but other means are also available such as teacher observation, pupil-teacher evaluation of the former's progress using recommended standards, portfolios, as well as using constructivism as a psychology of learning in the classroom. Then too, policy makers have a hangup of documentation of pupil achievement to track progress. Documentation, too frequently, means repetitious recording of test scores of pupils, over time. In contrast, voluntary test scores for each pupil might well be recorded to notice progress for a pupil over previous tests taken. A single test to determine promotion places too much stress on the learner as well as of the teacher. Any evaluation should answer the question, "Is the individual pupil achieving more optimally than previously?"

Quality Teaching and Learning

The standards movement seemingly does not take into account an important part of curriculum development and that is learning opportunities for pupils. Learning opportunities should assist pupils to attain objectives of instruction, but not necessarily the ones chosen by policy makers. Objectives need to be flexible and open ended. Pupil input here is also salient. Who is to say that policy makers have the holy grail to ascertain these ends? Certainly, pupil interests and purposes also have merit. Adults would not like to have dictated what is to be read, studied, and pursued in terms of goals in life. Thus, pupil interests must be a valuable consideration in learning opportunities in the classroom. Pupils as well as adults do better in life if they can pursue what is of interest. Learning opportunities can be made interesting and teachers must keep the interest factor in mind when choosing which learning opportunities pupils are to pursue.

Pupil purpose, too, is significant. Without purpose or reasons for learning, pupils achieve very little, generally. Building purpose for learning is time well spent in any lesson or unit of study. Thus, pupils need to perceive knowledge and skills as being relevant and having use in society. Perceiving the importance of what is being studied is vital. It is good if pupils can relate personally to content studied in the language arts, social studies, mathematics, and science. The scope needs to be broadened to include music, art, and physical education, rather that a narrow reading and mathematics emphasis as is presently the case. Multiple intelligences theory indicates that there is more to life than reading and mathematics. Pupils have talents and abilities in other curriculum areas, also.

Meaning must be emphasized, too, in ongoing activities. Learning activities then must make sense. Merely covering pages in a textbook and learners not attaching meaning to vital facts, concepts, and generalizations encountered wastes time and is costly in actual achievement. Rather, the following factors need consideration in teaching and learning :

- going from the known to the unknown
- perceiving sequence in learning
- relating content studied to the self, to others, as well as other vital ideas encountered.

When standards are set prior to instruction, are these salient to learners involved in their achievement? If not the teacher must attempt to induce saliency within learners. The standards movement comes from human beings who in return write objectives for pupil attainment. They should not be looked upon as being absolutes, in and of themselves, but rather consist of broad guidelines which give leeway to interpretation. Thus, there is flexibility in teacher decision making to adapt these and other objectives to where pupils are presently achieving. They also may need adjusting to harmonize with the entire school curriculum. A rigid form of behaviorism with its precise measurably stated objectives stresses a formal curriculum which tends to become factual in its leanings. Multiple choice test items appearing on high stakes testing have pupils zero in on knowledge to determine the correct response of four distractors. There is no room then for quality critical and creative thinking. The correct answer must then be identified within multiple choice test items. With critical thought, pupils analyze subject-matter before arriving at a conclusion. Then to with creative thinking, the learner comes up with unique ideas which are original and novel. Behaviorism leaves little room for thinking of alternatives, other than what is presented in a multiple choice test. Life does not consist of choosing from four given alternatives in a test, in order to make every day decisions.

Charter Schools

Charter schools are growing rapidly in number. Originally, charters were freed of many governmental regulations in order to experiment with better teaching ideas than those exemplified in the public schools. They are funded as a part of the moneys which otherwise would go entirely to the public schools. There are a plethora of charter schools and this makes it, indeed, difficult to say how innovative they are. And, if exempt from standards which apply to the public schools, it is difficult to ascertain if pupils truly do better in these schools.

There are a plethora of questions which need answering pertaining to charters :

- do public schools do less well when moneys are siphoned which go to charter schools?
- how can charters show effectiveness when they are freed from public school evaluations?
- why all the clamor for implementation of charter schools?
- why not improve present day public schools?
- how do they figure in with the turn around schools movement?

If selected governmental regulations are harmful to the public schools, why are these not done away with? Certainly, one does not want to implement what is harmful to pupils. How can comparisons then be made between charters and the public schools?

Closing the Gap in Achievement

Much is written about closing the gap in achievement between the dominant group and minorities. I gather this means, in my interpretation of the educational literature, to mean that the minority group must catch up and hold the dominant group to lower levels of progress. Each pupils needs to achieve as much as possible with high quality teachers, materials of instruction, and supervisory aid. Time and time again, research shows that schools do more poorly in poverty areas. Poverty hinders pupils from experiencing the good life with excellent library books in the home, visiting places of educational importance, taking vacations to nearby and remote areas, as well as different kinds of travel, among other possibilities. This indicates that much more must be done to eliminate/ minimize poverty. The late President Lyndon Johnson was greatly concerned about the evils of poverty with his Great Society emphasis. The view that anything done to benefit the lower income person is "socialist," or "communist" is absurd.

Each family must have quality and safe housing, adequate and nutritious food, and proper clothing. This should be a human right and considered to be humane. One person should not own one or more mansions with twin indoor swimming pools containing different temperature readings of water, and an eighteen hole golf course in a plush area of the city / country, while selected others are cold and hungry. Also, adequate health and dental care should be a right, not privilege, for everyone. These are salient for all pupils as well as well as adults to possess and do well in society.

How people are taxed by law will matter much in the amount of disposable income available to buy the good things in life. Laws whereby the upper income levels are given tax breaks as was done during the time a war is fought is not justifiable. Justifying these tax breaks on the basis of stimulating the economy is ridiculous. Fighting wars, too, should be discouraged, such as invading a nation due to false reports involving weapons of mass distraction. There is much which can be used to improve society if wars were not popular with selected groups of lay people. Fundamentalism is a cause for a plethora of wars and leads to extremism. Fighting wars is very expensive; there is much killing, wounding, maiming, and destruction of property. There can be bankruptcies of nations and demoralization as a result. Social programmes can thrive if the following exist :

- everyone pays taxes which are due to the different levels of government. Leona Helmsley's statement that only poor people pay taxes probably is true in too many cases. When cabinet positions were made to the recently elected president, the person designated Secretary of Health and Welfare had to step aside due to owing a hefty among of money to the federal government, something like $150,000. How many others are there who owe money to the federal government?
- advertisements were taken off the air by companies offering their services to reduce taxes for individuals.

It should definitely be made illegal to offer these "services." These commercial companies do not give examples of people who say that they are forced unjustly to pay a certain amount of tax moneys. One couple in the TV ad state they *owed* $3 million dollars and the commercial company assisted them in paying less than one million dollars in federal income tax.

- the statement that "Social Security will go bankrupt, and we all know it, by the year 2015" is definitely untrue, especially if taxes were paid above the $102,000 level of income. Why not extend the level of taxation upward indefinitely? Then there would be less need for hysteria and people who have the income will not suffer for paying more into Social Security. The two tier society of the wealthy and the poor needs rethinking in terms of what it means for a democracy.
- eliminating badly written legislation and adding what is fair. CEOs of huge corporations and large companies who receive huge salaries such as twenty million dollars a year with bonuses and stock options, even if a business enterprise is failing, is absurd and definitely unjustifiable.

Better laws need to be written and put into operation. Legislators need to be held accountable for unfortunate laws. Thus, one can bankrupt a corporation/company with huge salaries, excessive bonuses, and multiplicity of stock options and not commit a crime whereas in stealing a $5 package of meat, the involved person may be arrested, booked, and even imprisoned.

9

CHAPTER

Issues in School Curriculum

There are a plethora of issues in curriculum development which need resolving. These issues reveal diverse philosophies and psychologies of learning. Each side has merits as well as problems. Then too, perhaps, one side of an issue will be more appealing to an intellect than the other; this will be especially true in a democracy where diversity is prized in ideas presented. A brief analysis of each issue will be given.

An Analysis of Curricular Issues

There, no doubt, will be more issues than those presented in this writing. First, charter schools tend to be increasing greatly in number. When charters were first implemented, the emphasis was that these schools be innovative and free from unnecessary rules and regulations which govern the public schools. It almost sounded as if charters were to be experimental in nature. New ideas in teaching might then be tried out and publicized. The calls for accountability will make for a more uniform curriculum with that of the regular public schools. Accountability stresses testing to notice how well pupils are doing in achievement when progress is compared among and between individual school systems and states in the nation. Accountability, also, holds teachers responsible for pupil progress, based on test score results. For their operation, charter schools siphon moneys from public schools. There are several questions pertaining to charter schools :

- How is pupil performance appraised in charter schools when making comparisons with those in the public schools?
- Does money taken from public schools to run charters hinder pupil achievement in the former?
- has charter schools truly made for quality innovative procedures in teaching?
- if doing away with selected regulations for charters help learner achievement, why not do away with these same regulations in the public schools? (Ediger 2008).

Second, mandated testing to indicate pupil progress emphasizes sameness (standardization) in test items for all pupils on a particular grade level, sameness in time limits for all in test taking, sameness in directions for taking the test, among other facets of uniformity. "One size fits all," is a slogan to be used here: however, pupils differ from each in many ways such as ability, interests, and purposes, among other ways.

Teachers, here, may have written objectives to use as guidelines for teaching and learning situations. The objectives are the same for each grade level. Teachers need to teach and pupils need to learn what is in the objectives in order to pass the standardized, mandated test. Pupils may experience much drill, prior to test taking.

Toward the other end of the continuum is constructivism, a philosophy/psychology of instruction which stresses no drill and no mandated testing of pupils. Responsibility for learning resides with the individual learner. The teacher motivates, encourages, challenges, and facilitates achievement. Pupils are active participants in learning, not passive recipients of knowledge and skills. Lecture as a method of teaching is not emphasized; instead, learning by discovery is stressed. Here, pupils are guided to develop their very own concepts and generalizations. If a pupil has a question in an ongoing lesson, he/she is assisted through teacher questioning to arrive at a correct answer. If opinions are involved, pupils individually are to develop their own conclusions, based on knowledge, rational thought and decision making. It is the pupil who must do the learning and not the teacher. The teacher's role is to assist pupils to secure needed answers. Pupil ownership of the curriculum is important. In this way, constructivists believe that pupils optimize learning when it is self directed (Alam, 2009).

Pupils sequence their very own learnings when content is not understood; assistance from teachers in these teaching and learning situations makes for order in meaningful contextual situations. Building upon past learning experiences aids the pupil in bringing order to what is being acquired.

Third, selected educators believe in strict emphasis upon the academics in the school setting. Focusing on subject-matter content in the curriculum receives priority. Basal textbooks are utilized to provide major learnings for pupils. Objectives in the curriculum, for example, reflect the importance of the social sciences (history, geography, economics, and political science), mathematics (arithmetic, algebra, geometry, among others), English, and the natural sciences (biology, physics, chemistry, as well as the earth sciences). Art, music, and physical education are somewhat peripheral, Educators focusing upon the academics believe the academics provide a quality basis for general education in pursing further vocational, professional, and career ends. Mandated state objectives for pupil attainment presently emphasize content from the academics (Fitzhugh, 2006).

Toward the other end of the curriculum, an activity centered curriculum is stressed. Here, a more open ended curriculum is being stressed to meet individual pupil needs.

Thus, pupil/ teacher planning may be emphasized. Thus within an ongoing unit of study, pupils individually or collectively identify a problem. The problem requires deliberation and thought, not factual answers. Indepth learning from a variety of references sources are utilized to secure a tentative answer, resulting in an hypothesis. The hypothesis is subject to testing, and as a result, may be modified or refuted. New problems might well arise in these endeavors (Ford, 2008).

The role of the teacher in problem-solving activities encompasses being a guide, a resource person, and a motivator. The teacher does not lecture but, rather, helps pupils to locate necessary information to solve identified problems. With problem solving, pupils are :

- actively engaged in learning and not being passive recipients of knowledge and skills.
- ordering their own experiences and not following the dictates of the teacher.
- moving around in the classroom to locate reference sources of information.
- motivated by peers as well as the teacher in ongoing endeavors (Dewey, 1916).

Fourth, teaching toward having pupils achieve specific objectives is advocated by behaviorists as a psychology of learning. The objectives must be clearly stated so there is no guesswork as to what pupils are to learn. The objectives are stated prior to instruction and leave little/no leeway for flexibility. Learning activities are carefully aligned with the objectives so that each objective might be achieved by learners. Evaluation stresses if pupils did/did not achieve the objective being emphasized. Each of three components of the curriculum—objectives, learning opportunities, and evaluation procedures is closely structured and related.

Toward the other end of the continuum, a multi-media curriculum might be implemented for pupils to attain a flexible number of objectives. A variety of concrete, semi-concrete, and abstract experiences may be provided to stress in making provision for individual differences. These activities provide for different learning styles possessed by pupils. Thus, pupils may benefit from the learning opportunity which harmonizes best with an individual style'of learning. Self-evaluation by pupils may be used to ascertain achievement and progress. The teacher also uses diverse evaluation techniques including teacher observation along with teacher written tests to ascertain how well pupils are learning.

Fifth, selected educators emphasize the basics in the curriculum for all pupils to take as course work. Pupil achievement is considered important in mastering essential knowledge and skills. The basics represent a core of ideas which pupils must possess in order to do well in society. Abstract concepts and generalizations, coming from the basics, provide objectives for learner attainment. Advocates of the basics in the curriculum believe that core knowledge and skills are the best approach in preparing individuals for future occupations, jobs, and professions (Ediger, 2008).

To achieve essential subject-matter, pupils need to experience selected content appropriate for sequential grade levels. Pupils need to be tested frequently to notice if the basics are being attained. These essentials can be identified and be tested upon in multiple choice test items on mandated tests.

Toward the other end of the continuum, pupils may choose from several options, as determined by the teacher, what to learn. Choices are involved and the learner is the decision maker as to what meets personal interests,and purposes. They may also involve choosing between individual versus committee or collective endeavors. The pupil is to do the learning and must have an important role in making choices. If pupils can make decisions in terms of what to learn, they tend to make choices based on personal abilities and needs. Pupils achieve more optimally if they are actively involved in making selections in ongoing lessons and units of study, rather than being passive recipients of predetermined objectives to attain (Ediger, 2007).

Sixth, much of a pupil's school time is spent in the classroom, experiencing a basics curriculum or where choices are made in terms of what to learn and achieve. The former stresses more of what is to be accomplished in order to do well on mandated tests, while the latter philosophy is predicated on looking at the learner to ascertain meeting personal needs in the curriculum. Somewhat opposite, pupils may use the community to foster what is deemed useful in society for pupil learning. Resource personnel may then come into the classroom to talk about their specialty and use related AV aids in their presentation as it relates to a unit of study or a lesson. Pupils with teacher supervision may also visit a site in the community, relating it to previous learnings acquired. Real objectives from another culture may also be brought into a classroom and discussed. Learner questions need careful attention and may be used as follow ups to encourage project methods in subsequent activities. By relating the community to classroom experiences, pupils experience authenticity in learning. Using the community as a basis for learning may also be expanded with the following, among others :

- visits to nursing homes to present programs and interact with older people.
- doing age appropriate, safe community service projects.
- preparing/eating native food dishes as they relate to a selected culture being studied.
- making bird houses and feeders to notice bird migration in the out of doors.
- learning folk dances of another nation.

Seventh, technology is certainly seeing its many uses in teaching and learning situations. This includes online learning. There are baccalaureate, masters', and doctoral degrees offered by universities online. High school students are taking an increasing number of courses online. This, no doubt, will increase in number as kindergarten pupils are being introduced to working on the computer to solve math problems as well as to read library books thereon.

Online learning is very convenient to the student in that he/she may complete course work when convenient. When taking these courses at home, there is very little travel expense. Time is saved from traveling to a university campus and from traffic frustration that might well be spent in studying and completing courses. Quality needs to be insured in each course taken online. As is usually the case, there are also disadvantages :

- there is little time for interaction with the instructor and with peers.
- virtual reality is emphasized and authenticity tends to be lacking.
- the student must be well disciplined and motivated to pursue and complete online coursework.
- learning becomes highly abstract and lacks the concreteness, for example, of observing teachers at work.

More high quality research must be done to determine the effectiveness of online learning, as well as of each curriculum plan discussed.

References

Alam, Mahmood (2009), "Academic Achievement in Relation to Creativity and Achievement Motivation; A Correlational Study," *Edutracks*, 8(9), 31-34.

Dewey, John (1916), *Democracy and Education*, New York: The Macmillan Company.

Ediger, Marlow (2008), "Leadership in the School Setting," *Education*, 129(1), 17-20.

Ediger, Marlow (2007), "Teacher Observation to Assess Student Achievement," *Journal of Instructional Psychology*, 34 (3), 127-139.

Ediger, Marlow (2008), "Modern School Mathematics," *College Student Journal*, 42 (4), 986-989.

Fitzhugh, Will (2006), "Where's the Content?" *Educational Leadership*, 64 (2), 42-47.

Ford, Dennis (2008), "Student Success the Way They Need It: Powerful School Change," *Phi delta Kappan*, 90 (4), 281-291.

10

CHAPTER

Issues in Curriculum Improvement

There are two somewhat opposing psychologies in education which have stood the test of time in the school curriculum. One psychology was developed largely by E. L. Thorndike (1874-1949) who emphasized *behaviourism* as a school of thought in developing the curriculum with his precise behaviorally stated objectives. These objectives must be stated, prior to instruction, for pupils to achieve. Aligned tests to measure progress reveal what pupils have learned. The teacher is largely in control of classroom activities.

Toward the other end of the curriculum, John Dewey (1859-1952) stressed *experimentalism*, as a philosophical school of thought, with problem solving being a key component. Considerable pupil involvement is then emphasized in teaching and learning situations (Ediger and Rao, 2002).

Behaviourism Versus Experimentalism

Behaviorists believe strongly in the *measurement* concept with it strict emphasis upon obtaining numerical results from pupil achievement in terms of test scores. E. L. Thorndike advocated that "Anything which exists, exists in some amount, and if it exists in some amount, it can be measured." Thus, in any curriculum area, pupil progress can be measured to ascertain achievement. The following plans of testing emphasize behaviourism :

- mandated testing on the state level. The results are used to determine promotion of pupils to the next grade level, such as in grades three through eight and an exit test on the secondary level for graduation purposes.
- national tests to ascertain how well pupils are doing in achievement from year to year, such as the National Assessment of Educational Progress (NAEP).
- international tests to compare different nations in pupil achievement such as TIMSS (Third International Mathematics and Science Study) (Griffen 2004).

Characteristics of behaviourism include the following :

- precision in test results are provided such as a pupil being on the sixtieth percentile, meaning out of every one hundred pupils tested, forty are above and 60 below the sixtieth percentile.
- teachers teaching toward pupils achieving specific, precise objectives.
- pupils receiving the same directions for test taking, the same length of time for each test taken, and the same test items for the designated grade level of the test. Thus, all variables are the same, except for the pupils taking the test.
- multiple choice test items, generally, being on each test. These can be machine scored using the same answer key for each grade level test.
- print outs obtained from test results indicating the percentile, grade equivalent, stanine, or age equivalent of the test taker.
- test results also indicate which test items were missed. This provides a basis for review/new objectives for pupil attainment.

With behaviourism, there is a very close connection among objectives, learning activities, and appraisal results. Cognitive objectives are the main stay of behaviourism. These objectives must be carefully sequenced so that pupil success is in the offing. Learning activities are focused upon pupils achieving the specific ends. Teachers need to be educated and trained to teach for pupils achieving the specific objectives, only. Evaluation stresses the importance of tests measuring what is contained in the precise objectives of instruction. Guess work is taken out of the equation with behaviorism as a psychology of instruction due to interaction among the objectives, learning activities, and appraisal procedures. An exact numeral is provided for pupils' test results and these may be compared with test results of other learners in the same grade level. Yearly progress is reported based on test results for each pupil, with comparisons also made among schools, school districts and states (Ediger, 2008).

Toward the other end of the continuum, experimentalism is emphasized with problem-solving procedures as one approach. In an ongoing lesson or unit of study, pupils with teacher guidance identify a problem. The problem is clearly stated and based on pupil interests and purposes. Encouragement provides effort in pupil problem selection. Pupils need to do the learning and be active participants in the curriculum. The teacher serves as a resource person, helper, and assistant (Dewey, 1916).

The learning process moves forward with pupils securing necessary information in problem solving with an hypothesis or tentative answer to the stated problem. Diverse reference sources are used such as concrete (excursions, objects, items, quality resource personnel, among others), semi-concrete (illustrations, video tapes, power point presentations, computer sources, among others), and abstract materials (basal textbooks, library books, magazines, newspaper articles, as well as other print materials). Pupils choose which reference sources provide needed information in answer to the problem. Learners engage with learning activities as they relate to individual differences, personal background information of participants, as well as those engaged in through scaffolding.

Information obtained require pupils to work collectively in problem-solving and is a dynamic procedure. Respect for each other and for ideas obtained are musts. Ideas will need to be harmonized within a committee setting. Progress in problem solving comes from pupils accepting each other in a democratic setting.

Answers to the problem, from information secured, test the hypothesis. Learning is an active process, and pupils with teacher guidance order their very own experiences in gathering subject-matter as well as in testing an hypothesis. Pupils discover concepts and generalizations; they are not told answers to questions, but discover, through effort, needed content. Meaning and understanding occurs through interaction with others. Pupils interact with each other and with the teacher in problem solving situations. Sequence, ultimately, resides within the learner and not within the materials of instruction.

Problem-solving also emphasizes one form of constructivism whereby the latter stresses the following :

- active involvement of learners in developing ongoing lessons and units of study.
- pupils working collaboratively in the curriculum.
- pupils interact with the teacher as in a dynamic social situation.
- evaluation stresses pupils working together with the teacher to improve learning situations.
- pupils guided to find their own answers to problems and questions.
- knowledge and skills are holistic and not factual, nor in isolated parts (Everhart, 2009).

In addition to problem solving, there are additional approaches in stressing experimentalism whereby pupils have a large voice in ascertaining what to learn. *William Heard Kilpatrick* (1874-1965) emphasized a project method whereby pupils were wholeheartedly involved in also sequencing their own experiences. Here, pupils completed a project with an authentic procedure of constructing something concrete in nature (Ediger and Rao, 2003). The following general sequence may be followed by pupils with teacher assistance :

- *Pupil purposing.* There needs to be a purpose in doing a project. These purposes come from the learner.
- *Pupil planning.* Here, pupils collectively in a small group develop ordered, flexible steps for proceeding with the project.
- *Pupil executing or carrying out the plans to fruition.*
- Pupil judging the completed project in terms of desired criteria.

With Dr. Kilpatrick's project method, pupils are active learners, not passive recipients of knowledge. The teacher's role is to help, assist, and guide, but not lecture. Pupil ownership of the curriculum is definitely in evidence. Within small groups of four to five pupils, there is peer interaction with support from the teacher. Quality interaction among committee members is salient as is the quality of the finished project.

Experimentalism is very much in vogue today with the following plans of instruction also being stressed by teachers :

- *Peer mediated instruction.* Here, pupils work together on an activity with discussions ongoing until the task is completed. For example in reading, peers may agree upon a selection to be read and then, indepth, answer agreed upon questions and problems, collaboratively.
- *Pupil planning* of a creative dramatics presentation from a history lesson/unit of study with agreed upon parts played by individuals in making history come live.
- Reader's theater in which pupils individually practice reading aloud a play performance. Intonation of voice,

pitch, accent, and juncture play important roles for each read aloud. The final presentation may be presented to other classrooms of pupils. There is considerable cooperation in planning such as who gets which play part and how the read aloud is to be given orally. Rehearsals are necessary for a good presentation.

IN SUMMARY

Two somewhat opposing schools of thought were presented in curriculum development. Behaviourism emphasizes precise objectives be established for pupil achievement. Either pupils do/do not attain these objectives as a result of teaching. Experimentalism, in contrast, stresses that objectives tend to arise as a lesson/unit of study progresses. Problem-solving, as one example, emphasizes that pupils identify a problem and work collectively toward a solution. Pupils, here, with teacher guidance develop the curriculum with somewhat heavy pupil involvement.

REFERENCES

Dewey, John (1916), *Democracy and Education.* New York; The Macmillan Company.

Ediger, Marlow, and D. Bhaskara Rao (2002), *Psychology and Curriculum.* New Delhi, India: Discovery Publishing House.

Ediger, Marlow, and D. Bhaskara Rao (2003), Philosophy and the Curriculum. New Delhi, India: Discovery Publishing House.

Ediger, Marlow (2008) "The American High School," College Student Journal, 42 (3), 814-817.

Everhart, Jerry (2009), "You Tube in the classroom," *Science and Children*, 46 (9), 32-25.

Griffen, Sharon (2004), "Teaching Number Sense," *Educational Leadership*, 61 (5), 39-42.

11

CHAPTER

Problems in Curriculum Development

There are selected problems in curriculum development which need to be resolved. These problems relate to pupil learning in ongoing units of study and involve what is relevant and salient to learn. Determining revisions and modifications in curriculum development need to be continuous and ongoing. As pupils and society change, so must the school curriculum. The curriculum of the past is no longer useful presently. Thus, which changes and modifications need to be made in the curriculum?

Curriculum Trends

A major change which must be made pertains to what is significant for pupil learning. With emphasis having been placed upon mandated objectives of instruction, teachers have been pressured to teach what will be tested. Reading and mathematics then have received primary attention. High stakes testing stresses that each pupil pass a mandated test to be promoted to the next higher grade level. This leaves out selected curriculum areas. Science has just recently been added to the mandated areas for testing, but it still leaves out others which are highly important (Ediger, 2008).

Test results should compare a pupil's present achievement with his/her past measurable achievement to notice progress. This is salient for parents to notice achievement of a son/ daughter from one time to the next. Also, diagnostic results must indicate what teachers and parents need to provide assistance in, so that sequential progress may be in the offing for the pupil (Ediger, 2008).

The most important objectives for pupil attainment may not be emphasized in the curriculum. These include the following :

- caring for the welfare of others, especially those who have disabilities
- assisting others in need; this also stresses helping pupils academically as the need arises
- working cooperatively with others in a project related to an ongoing unit of study
- wanting to do quality work in school and in society
- being a good citizen by helping to improve the human condition in society (Sapon-Shevin, 2008).

The asterisked items listed above are difficult to emphasize in teaching and learning situations as well as being difficult to ascertain and measure pupil achievement and progress therein. To begin with, the teacher may serve as a model in caring, assisting, and working cooperatively. He/ she should call attention in class of pupils showing specific acts involving these behaviors. As much as possible, these kinds of objectives need to be stressed in ongoing lifelike situations. Merely memorizing traits of good behavior is not adequate! A doing approach is much superior.

Attitudinal Objectives

There are salient objectives which need to be emphasized, but are not in the realm of mandated tested nor can they be classified as subject matter. These come under the *attitudes* heading. For example, "empathy" is such a concept which may be stated as an objective for pupil attainment. Thus, learning of academic content, by itself, is to be prized, but it leaves out how an individual relates to others. Empathy stresses :

- possessing positive feelings towards others
- having consideration for people and their accomplishments
- being able to 'step into the shoes' of others and understand their feelings
- understanding how negative teasing hurts others
- frowning upon rudeness, harassment, gossip, and intimidation.

Pupil achievement is hindered when negative statements are made to and about others. For example, pupils may fear coming to school when harassment is in evidence, or learners become timid when intimidation is present. The writer when supervising university student teachers in the public schools noticed numerous cases of harassment such as a pupil :

- kicking another child under the classroom desk after sharpening his pencil
- hitting another learner after returning to his seat from asking a question of the teacher
- ridiculing an answer given by a pupil
- being extremely rude with remarks made to a child when going out to recess
- rubbing a pupil's ears, when no one was watching, until they were red, while waiting for the school bus (Crawford, 2008).

Our fifth grade son cried at home one evening when his mother noticed black spots on his ankles. He finally said what had happened. A bully on the school bus would kick his ankles if he did not pay money to avoid the terror. Our son feared grave repercussions if his mother and I would tell the bus driver or the director of school transportation of these happenings. We went to the director of school transportation in this city of 18,000 people and told him what had happened and our son's repercussion fears. The director was very empathetic and said this would not happen again and to not fear any consequences. It worked! There was no more terror money paid to the perpetrator of the kicking and he behaved perfectly on the school bus the rest of the school year. It is extremely difficult for parents to know what to do in these cases. If it had not worked, we had an alternative plan in mind to resolve the conflict. The director of school transportation, or other authorized person, must act quickly; there is no time for continuous bruising to occur.

Rules to curtail harassing need to be clear and must be communicated to pupils, teachers, and school administrators. There need to be immediate penalties and punishments due the transgressor. These need to be spelled out with clarity. To harass is not good for the harasser; it builds a negative self image. To receive any kind of 'reward' for harassing hinders in achieving good will and a positive self image. Harassing can only bring on bad consequences as this act continues. Who knows what the receiver of the harassment will do to the perpetrator? It is best, of course, to avoid any of these happenings to occur.

A third problem in curriculum development pertains to the need for cooperation. Too frequently, competition has been the rule of the day when the only good is for a child to outdo the other. Thus, it is imperative that pupils learn to work together for the common good of all in a classroom. Extreme cases of competition may result in :

- cheating to get ahead of others in academic classroom tests, copying a report as one's own on a selected topic from a computer printout, and giving excuses (lying) for assignments not completed
- paying others to do one's class assignments
- threatening others to not "work as hard" thus lowering class standards for the former to get ahead

- tripping others on the playground and in class. There are numerous cases whereby a pupil sticks his/her leg out to trip others who go to the teacher's desk for assistance or to sharpen a pencil. Feelings of embarrassment hinder pupil achievement and progress. So often, too, feelings of revenge come about in these situations (Merwin, 2005).

Classroom rules need to be established which stress quality work habits and these must become a part of the repertoire of the pupil. A major rule should be that pupils do not say or do anything mean to others. Examples of this rule and other rules need to be given so that each truly understands mean behavior which includes harassment. It must be discussed meaningfully how negative behavior hinders others from achieving as optimally as possible. Humiliation does not make for positive feelings or for friendship making (Ediger, 2007).

Subject-matter Learnings

Academic content needs to be relevant and possesses practical usage. Learning content for the sake of doing so will not be too encouraging to most learners. In the study of history, pupils need to draw conclusions as to what can be used presently from learnings of the past. For example, in studying units on world history the fighting of wars not only bankrupted nations but also caused tremendous damage to moral judgements. Deaths in combat, loss of limbs, brain damage, and mental illness, resulted from wars along with property/land damage. Incorporated skills include problem solving, critical and creative thinking (Dash, 2008).

Project methods may be stressed in ongoing units of study such as pupils with teacher guidance :

- developing a model village in a region prior to and after involved armed forces inflicted damages
- an agricultural area showing luscious farm crops followed by sequential illustrations showing their destruction, as a result of war

- doing a model refugee camp for those having lost homes from armed conflict.

There are a plethora of possibilities when pupil/teacher planning is involved. Ample input from the learner is necessary based on background knowledge possessed. The following are considerations for pupil/teacher planning :

- interests involved in doing a specific project
- maturity level of the learner
- meaningful learning being accrued in that the project must make sense as well as possess purpose
- the learning style of the pupil in preferring individual versus committee endeavors (See Ness, 2007).

The planned and completed project may be shown within the classroom with other classes being invited to view the displays. Questions may then be asked by viewers. These questions might well provide fodder for more indepth studies. Personal initiative is salient in doing projects.

IN CLOSING

Curriculum development involves much planning in terms of objectives for pupils to attain, learning opportunities to achieve the objectives, and evaluation procedures to ascertain achievement and progress. There are diverse kinds of activities for learner engagement to achieve, develop, and grow. This includes technology use. Regardless of the mode of instruction, pupils must understand what is taught, be fully engaged in learning, perceive value in achieving, and be able to apply facts, concepts, and generalizations acquired.

REFERENCES

Crawford, Marilyn (2008), "Thinking Inside the Clock," *Phi Delta Kappan*, 90(4), 251-255.

Dash, Neena (2008), "Decision-Making in Schools," *Edutracks*, 8(4), 10-12.

Ediger, Marlow (2008), "The School and Students in Society," *Journal of Instructional Psychology*, 35 (3), 260-263.

Ediger, Marlow (2008), "Leadership in the School Setting," *Education*, 129(1), 17-20.

Ediger, Marlow (2007), "Preparing School Administrators," *Reading Improvement*, 44 (3), 149-152.

Merwin, Michelle Marks (2005), "On Being Respected or Liked: Principle Centered Teaching," *College Student Journal*, 39 (4), 798-805.

Ness, Molly (2007), "Reading Comprehension Strategies in Secondary Content-Area Classrooms," *Phi Delta Kappan*, 89 (3), 229-231.

Sapon-Shevin, Mara, "Learning in an Inclusive Community," *Educational Leadership*, 66 (1), 49-53.

12

CHAPTER

Career Education and Curriculum

Career education is important for students in that each will ultimately select a career option. Careers chosen need to be of interest. A boring job makes for a lack of satisfaction and may be perceived as a dead end position. There are then few opportunities for promotion or an adequate level of income to raise a family. Career satisfaction is salient. It is significant to feel that what one does is worthy in society. Contributions are then made to improve conditions in the societal arena. Positive attitudes need to be developed toward work and society. Being a contributing member makes for feelings of self worth whereby esteem needs tend to be met. Feelings of adequacy should prevail in any career chosen. Then too, possessing feelings of belonging minimizes a belief in being alone in this world. Individuals need to feel they belong to an organization, a club, family of classmates, and to a community (Ediger, 2007).

Unit Teaching and Career Education

When should units on careers be emphasized? There are a plethora of opportunities when students enter school. Careers selected should be relevant, authentic, enduring, and positive.

On the pre-school/kindergarten level, developmentally appropriate library books may be read to young learners on a variety of salient careers. The illustrations therein must be viewed by pupils as the read aloud continues. It is salient for the teacher to read with proper stress, pitch and enunciation. Using a quality voice assists students to be actively involved while listening to the read aloud.

In addition to library books in the read aloud, the teacher may also show illustrations of people at the work place. A clear view of each illustration is important. Young children need to make comments and raise questions on their understanding level pertaining to the illustrations. Also, a power point presentation on any grade/age level may capture learner attention on careers. The presentation needs to be at a pace which makes for maximum student attention and understanding. Each frame in the power point presentation must present information on a relevant career. Engaged learners need to identify questions which stimulate a discussion. Clarification of subject-matter discusses is important. Proper procedures in conducting a discussion need to be followed whereby each participant's comments and questions are respected and rudeness is outlawed (Parker, 2001).

Library books need to deal with different careers and be on diverse reading levels. Individual differences among learners need adequate provision. Self-selection of library books needs to be encouraged. The teacher may desire to evaluate student comprehension of subject matter from each book read. A random sampling of students may provide this necessary information. Thus, the teacher may ask a student at his/her desk to say aloud a few major ideas read from a completed library book. The evaluation could be more extensive in that the teacher has a conference with a student after each library book on careers has been completed in silent reading to check comprehension. Also, the student may read aloud a selection from the library book on careers to the teacher to ascertain the quality of word recognition and identification. The teacher might then record what was observed and refer to the recordings prior to the next sequential conference. The goal should be to have students learn more about careers regardless of the kind of evaluation procedure used. Enjoyment of reading on careers should be an end result (Ediger, 2008).

Library book content may be used in classroom discussions. They may be used along with power point presentations as well as the basal textbook. When questions and problems are identified in classroom discussions, students may respond with what has been acquired from the different reference sources. Flexibility in sources used adds variety to ideas being considered. Students generally select reading materials based on personal interests and the appropriateness of the reading level of materials used. During the discussion in class, the personal interests on careers of the student may be elaborated upon by participants who present ideas pertaining to information read. Pictorial representations of each career adds to the clarity and meaning of each (March, 2005).

A university student teacher, supervised by the writer, encouraged parents to talk about and bring objects used in their personal careers to the classroom setting. The invitation list was later extended to other people in society who desired to share career information. The following, among others, participated in sharing information about their careers :

- a retired teacher and a retired school administrator
- an automobile mechanic and a carpenter
- an interior decorator and a carpet installer
- a nurse and an occupational therapist
- a piano instructor and a music teacher
- a manager of the produce department of a super market
- a representative from a super market.

Those participating in presenting information about their careers needed to bring along illustrations and concrete materials, if possible, pertaining to tools of the trade. Careful preparation and clear, interesting speaking voices add to each presentation. Questions from learners need encouragement. The questions may deal with needed training to enter a career. Also, students may wish to ask questions about the likes and dislikes of each career. A notice of criteria for effective presenters needs to be sent home with children or e-mailed to volunteers. Not all volunteers should come at the same time, but scheduled at appropriate intervals to facilitate student sequential learning in the classroom (Parish and Baker, 2006).

There are several ways of organizing the career education curriculum. Many teachers use a separate subjects approach whereby specific units on careers are taught. Advantages here are that students are assisted to focus upon one topic and that being *careers*. The careers chosen for emphasis need to be relevant and on the understanding level of students. Knowledge, skills, and attitudinal ends selected zero in on what is significant for students to know about careers. The learning activities chosen for students to achieve the stated objectives need to be varied and provide for individual differences. Diverse evaluation procedures may be selected to assist learners to find out what is known and what is left to know. A diagnostic approach is then stressed in that students have ample opportunities to study what was not understood as a result of the evaluation process. The scope or breadth of content deals with careers only (Henderson, 1995).

A second approach is to plan a correlated career education unit of study. Here, career education is brought into a unit of study as it relates directly to the ongoing subject matter taught. Thus, if a unit is taught on the souther states, only those vocations are selected for teaching that deal with that geographical area being taught. Relating of subject-matter taught is salient here. Students tend to remember facts, concepts, and generalizations better if they perceive their relationships. The scope or breadth of content in the correlated approach has been broadened to include other subject matter than careers only. The objectives, learning activities to achieve the objectives, and the evaluation procedures reflect a correlated curriculum (Ediger, 2007).

Regardless of how the curriculum is organized, the following additional learning activities are recommended :

- problem-solving procedures whereby an individual or committee identify a salient problem pertaining to careers, develop an hypothesis, and assess the hypothesis using a variety of worthwhile experiences.
- visiting work places which stress important and enduring careers, these excursions need careful planning for educational and safety values.
- simulate working in a career after adequate background information has been acquired. Have classmates critique and ask questions for clarification of the work involved.
- discussing education and training necessary for choosing a relevant career.
- selecting a favoured task on careers from a classroom learning station and doing an indepth study on that chosen career. Present acquired information individually to the entire class or to a small group of peers (The National Council on Economic Education, 1997).

There are definite economic concepts which may be studied by students in career education units of study. These identified concepts should help students to understand the world of work more fully. Many careers provide *goods*. Goods are concrete, useful items such as clothing, food items, building materials, ranges, refrigerators, clothes washers, and driers. To experience the concept of "goods," students should list goods they purchased recently. *Services* are those things which provide assistance or help given to others. They include paid services such as the work performed by teachers, policemen, firemen, plumbers, carpenters, auto-mobile mechanics, barbers, doctors, and lawyers. Students need to discuss services recently purchased such as a boy having secured a hair cut. *Opportunity benefits* stress such things as the advantages of following a certain line of work such as being a manager of a store. What are the advantages of being in a certain career? Opposite is the concept opportunity costs. Opportunity costs emphasize disadvantages of being in any career. It is important for students to study both the advantages and disadvantages of diverse careers. This provides a framework for making choices on future careers. Selected careers require much education, longer working hours, and/are more strenuous as compared to others. Possible salary differentials and earning power are also salient considerations in making a career choice.

Additional economic concepts which subsequently assist students in understanding the economic arena include the following :

- wants and needs
- the use of technology and computers as well as manual labor in the world of work
- assembly lines and mass production
- production, distribution, and consumption
- markets and competition
- scarcity, and the law of supply and demand
- profit, savings, and incentives
- banks, savings, and entrepreneurship (Rodgers *et al.*, 2007).

Each of the above may be listed as one or more objectives for students to attain. Learning opportunities may be chosen for students to achieve these objectives. Evaluation may follow to ascertain what students had learned.

References

Ediger, Marlow (2007), "The School and Students in Society," *Experiments in Education*, 35 (9), 17-20.

Ediger, Marlow (2008), "Mental Health in the Curriculum," *Journal of Instructional Psychology*, 35 (1), 38-42.

Ediger, Marlow (2007), "Meaning in the Reading Curriculum," *Reading Improvement*, 44 (4), 217-220.

March, Tom (2005), "The New WWW: Whatever, Whenever, Wherever," *Educational Leadership*, 65 (4), 14-19.

Henderson, W. (1995), *Economics in Literature*. London, England: Routledge.

Parish, Thomas S. and Brad Baker (2006), "An Attempt to Assist Student Athletes to Succeed in Various Ways, A Pilot Study," *College Student Journal*, 40 (4), 781-784.

Parker, Walter C. (2001), *Social Studies in Elementary Education*. Upper Saddle River, New Jersey : The Macmillan Company.

Rodgers, *et al.* (2007). "Teaching Economic Concepts Through Children's Literature in the Primary Grades," *The Reading Teacher*, 61 (1), 46-55.

National Council on Economics Education (1997), *Voluntary National Content Standards in Economics*. New York: NCEE.

13

CHAPTER

Co-curricular Activities and Student

There are a plethora of values involved for students who take an active role in co-curricular activities. These values compliment a well adjusted person and stress wholeness in human development. Classes taken such as in the fine and practical arts, the humanities, the social sciences, the natural sciences, mathematics, and physical education, provide objectives to be achieved in general education. These provide opportunities for students to explore knowledge and skills in a variety of academic and non-academic areas. They give students a chance to experience the world of knowledge/ abilities from diverse perspectives in which choices may be made for future vocations, avocations, hobbies, and interests.

Still, a student needs to select and make decisions about co-curricular experiences which might well harmonize with the standard curriculum. Which kinds of experiences should be open for learner choice? These may be labeled as co-curricular, and might well be based upon student interest, purpose, and meaning (Morgan and Williams, 2007).

Values of Co-curricular Activities

Faculty members and administrators need to study and assess

possible co-curricular areas with the intent of providing rich and satisfying experiences for students which harmonize with the regular curriculum. Values then of co-curricular experiences must be identified through surveys of students, interviews, as well as through problem solving approaches.

A major value of co-curricular experiences is for students to select that which is interesting. Interests propel the student to learn about possibilities for enrichment. Motivation is salient in selecting co-curricular activities, indepth learning may well occur in these situations. The knowledge and skills secured may also relate well to what is being studied in ongoing units of study in the classroom. Students then might be guided to appreciate the usual curriculum areas of the school. Co-curricular experiences may also open doors to possible vocations and avocations. Or, enduring leisure time experiences, too, might well also accrue. Leisure time should enrich and motivate the learner and not be wasted in useless activities (Reeves, 2008).

Second, friendships are developed through persons of like interests.The friendships may be enduring. They may well assist in learning in a co-curricular experience. Cooperative learning might be stressed whereby students harmonize efforts to come up with goal attainment. Learning to work cooperatively with others is a lifelong skill to develop and is useful in the classroom as well as at the future work place. Making friends and working collectively are indeed worthwhile and enduring ideals (Rena, 2008).

If competition is involved in the co-curricular activity, then participants need to accept winning humbly and defeat gracefully. These outcomes translate well into life in society. Both winning and losing, as well as in between points, are experienced by all. Co-curricular experiences should assist students to accept life as it is with its joys and disappointments. But, at the same time, much effort must be put forth to do well in life's endeavors. Resilience emphasizes bouncing back if disappointments are experienced. There is always another time and place to excel. It makes it possible to feel that disappointments are usually temporary and new opportunities accrue (Ediger, 2007).

Third, co-curricular activities provide opportunities to experience relevance in life, important activities abound and need to be sought, resulting in choices made. Students must experience what is significant in life. Co-curricuiar activities may well provide relevancy. By choosing to join an organization, the student through decisions i made pinpoints that which is salient. In meetings held for the club/ organization joined, the learner may make suggestions as to what he/she would like to see in ensuing programs, thus fostering relevancy. In this way, the student has input and develops feelings of belonging. Feelings of belonging are an important desire of i individuals. Any co-curricular experience needs to assist its members to develop bonds of cohesion within the framework of knowledge or skills being stressed. There are expectations of students pertaining to any organization. As much as possible, learners need to experience these expectations (Ediger, 2008a&b).

Fourth, co-curricular activities assist students to explore hobbies, talents, and abilities. This should result in selecting a desired leisure type activity. One of the goals of the Seven Cardinal Principles of Education (National Education Association, 1917) emphasized the wise use of leisure time. Leisure time is available to most individuals and each person must use it wisely. Wise use of leisure time stresses the importance of doing things which are uplifting, fulfilling, and pleasant. It provides for a change of activities to that which is truly enriching. From the change of pace involving co-curricular experiences, the student generally is ready to return to the studying of solid academic content.

It may be difficult to think of new things to do in one's spare time; however, co-curricular activities suggest relevant options to the routine. Self fulfilment may come about due to placing the emphasis upon novel things to do. Co-curricular experiences open new doors to do that which makes for creativity. Individuals like to engage in what make for the creative being. It loosens the grips on human beings to explore the novel and bring about originality. Students, in a plethora of situations, should have opportunities to look into unique situations and do that which might make for originality in product or process. Creativity is wanted in numerous situations in life since new ways of doing things have made for progress in society. The "tried and true" too frequently are emphasized and they fail to make for headways in solving of problems. A rich imagination may shed light on new knowledge (Ediger, 2008a&b).

Fifth, co-curricular experiences might well lead to an open mindedness to pursue new knowledge. Curiosity in the ongoing may be the motivator to pursue vital ideals in a new academic field. Co-curricular stresses the possibility of acquiring ideas through self selection and reflection. To monitor one's own thoughts and evaluate what has transpired provides opportunities to look back at what has been learned and relate these learnings to the new and ensuing academic fields of endeavors (Kumar, 2006).

Selecting Specific Co-curricular Activities

Quality leadership is needed to develop specific co-curricular activities for students. Perhaps, one needs to start organizing the co-curricular curriculum by analyzing what is being offered presently. A carefully devised survey may then be prepared and sent/handed to learners. From the survey, the sponsors may assess what students are interested in and would pursue. Students might also be interviewed in receiving input. A sincere effort needs to be made to ascertain these interests. Modifications may then be made in terms of offerings and changes which need to be made within each activity. Meeting student needs are vital in the co-curricular curriculum. They may be based upon multiple intelligences theory of learning.

Thus, the following multiple intelligences (Gardner, 1993) need consideration :

- **verbal intelligence :** A literary club, for example, may be initiated and students would decide which selections to embrace and discuss at different meetings. Large and small groups may be formed for these discussions. Creative dramatizations may be developed/presented pertaining to a literary selection.
- **logical intelligence :** Among other academic disciplines, mathematics stresses the use of logic to reason solutions. Here, students may work on developmentally appropriate math problems which spur student interest and purpose.
- **musical/rhythmical intelligence** may stress music appreciation, writing lyrics, and music, as well as perform diverse dance activities.
- **intrapersonal intelligence** whereby the student prefers to work by the self and this may involve doing a self selected project. Effort must be involved in producing a quality project.
- **interpersonal intelligence** whereby a student excels by engaging in group work. Standards of excellence are in evidence in doing a cooperative project.
- **bodily/kinesthetic intelligence** whereby a student excels in manual dexterity. Athletic endeavors may be stressed here as well as constructing objects and items in terms of desired criteria.
- **scientific intelligence** which emphasizes doing science experiments whereby the methods of science are stressed.

Each of the above intelligences may be expanded to meet student needs as well as encompass learner interests. Co-curricular activities should be engaging and purposeful. A sound theoretical foundation should be the basis for developing a quality co-curriculum set of experiences. There need to be choices which students may make in selecting that which satisfies. At one science fair judged by the writer, a student's project consisted of making a solar collector; the project grew out of interests developed in a science club, a co-curricular activity (Ediger, 2003).

References

Ediger, Marlow (2003), "Teacher Involvement to Evaluate Achievement," *Education*, 124 (1), 137-142.

Ediger, Marlow (2007), "The School and Students in Society," *Experiments in Education*, 35 (9), 188-190.

Ediger, Marlow (2008a), "Training Staff to Teach Reading Across the Curriculum," Leadership Compass, 5 (3), 1, 2.

Ediger, Marlow (2008b), "The American High School," *College Student Journal*, 42 (3), 814-817.

Gardner, Howard (1993), *Multiple Intelligences: Theory Into Practice.* New York: Basic Books.

Kumar, G. N. Smith (2006), Values of Co-Curricular Activities as Perceived Higher Secondary Students. Ph D thesis assessed by the writer as a Member of the External Evaluation Committee for St. Xavier College of Education, Palayamkottai, India, p. 17.

Morgan, Denise, and Jeffery L. Williams (2007), "Chapter Glancing: Noticing and Naming Chapter Openings," *The Reading Teacher*, 61 (2), 168-171.

National Education Association (1918), *Cardinal Principals of Secondary Education Bulletin.* Commission on the Reorganization of Secondary Education, pp. 32.

Reeves, Douglas B. (2008), "The Leadership Challenge in Literacy," *Educational Leadership*, 65 (7), 91-92.

Rena, Ravinder (2008), "Value-based Education for Human Development-Eritrean Perspective," *Edutracks*, 7 (11), 21-23.

14

CHAPTER

Psychology of Testing and Evaluation

Much emphasis is being placed upon testing as a means of determining what pupils have learned in school. *Behaviourism* is emphasized here with its measurement philosophy of determining what pupils have acquired. State mandated tests are used to ascertain what pupils have learned and achieved when comparing one state with another in the union. These test results may also be utilized in contrasting school districts in pupils making progress, or lack thereof, from one school year to the next. The National Assessment of Educational Progress (NAEP) is given to a representative set of students in the United States each year in comparing cohorts from one school year to the next. Then too, there are international comparisons among nations such as the Third International Mathematics and Science Study (TIMSS). Behaviorism, as a psychology of learning is being stressed with its measurable results given in numerical terms.

Toward the other side of the equation is *constructivism* which does not depend upon test results to ascertain pupil achievement. Constructivism emphasizes pupils learning by discovery which does not permit testing at each specific, flexible step of learning. In fact, tests are unimportant. Teacher observation can be a major approach in evaluating progress and achievement (Ediger and Rao, 2003).

Behaviorism and Measurement

Since the early 1900s, behaviourists have had a strong backing in measuring pupils in different areas of achievement. E. L. Thorndike (1874-1949) and associates developed standardized tests to measure curricular achievement in arithmetic, spelling, and reading, among others. Arithmetic is an accurate science in that there are exact answers in addition, subtraction, multiplication, and division, among other operations on number. Behaviourism can work well in these situations with the use of multiple choice test items where there is only one right answer of four plausible distractors to choose from. In the spelling of English words, there usually is a correct way of spelling a word. However, there are exceptions: catalog, catalogue.

Presently, there are many areas in which measurement philosophy is used including personality tests, vocational aptitude and interest tests, power tests, analogy tests, tests which predict success in a given endeavor, among a plethora of others. Testing has become a major enterprise with companies and corporations making hugh profits from developing and selling tests (Brady, 2008).

Validity is a very important concept in testing. A test then needs to measure what it purports to measure. It does take much money and time to develop any test such as one, for example, which claims to measure readiness for reading. There are problems in determining validity, such as in the area of teaching social studies. Names, dates, and places lend themselves well for test items in history as do many facts. The following are not that concise to measure in the social studies :

- evaluating qualities of good citizenship
- respecting others as well as caring for others

- good human relations
- self realization and its component parts (Ediger, 2008).

Attempts, of course, have been made to measure these more abstract and general concepts.

In addition to validity, reliability is a second major concept to stress in measurement, whereby a test measures consistently for any trait such, as readiness for reading. To determine reliability, the following procedures are used test/retest, alternate forms, split half, and/or a combination of these approaches. In using personality tests, the following can vary much, for example, in test/retest situations :

- how pupils feel toward school as well as toward the teacher, from one testing to the next
- how pupils react to each academic discipline in time.

The feeling dimension may vary considerably from one time to the next. Fatigue, an unhappy experience, and unfavorable testing environment enter into the equation. The writer when taking a standardized test at a university experienced a crowded room with no air conditioning at that time. The worst part was an adjacent student chewing gum loudly! Cognitive learnings are more stable as compared to the affective dimension, but even then forgetting occurs or learnings become hazy (Ediger, 2009).

Behaviourism, also includes master learning in that pupils achieve predetermined objectives. These objectives, developed prior to instruction, are the targets the teacher aims toward when choosing learning activities for pupils. Testing and measuring will ascertain if these objectives have been attained. The assumption is that once the test results indicate objectives have been achieved, then learning has occurred in the desired direction. There are several problems here :

- how stable are these learnings and does forgetting soon occur?
- how relevant are the objectives in terms of future use for learners? They appear to be absolutes and written in stone.

- how might pupils be involved in the curriculum? Behaviourism permits little leeway here (Ahmad 2009).
- are there better approaches in determining pupil achievement as compared to traditional testing? The optometrist mentioned above was not able to determine correct reading glasses by using the latest in technology.
- should pupils show more of their sequential learnings directly such as in discussions in all curriculum areas, reading aloud, use of arithmetic from daily assignments and from functional use of number, doing science experiments, engaging in the complete act of thought in problem solving, written work in each subject matter field, higher levels of cognition (critical and creative thinking, drawing inferences, cause/effect, as well as comparison/contrast).
- should diversity in evaluation be shown with pupils making drawings, diagrams, charts, and graphs to reveal what has been learned? (Teale and Campbell, 2007).

The above listed asterisked items indicate that multiple choice test items would not be used, but teacher observation might well take its place. However, the accountability movement wants data, generally standardized test results, to show pupil progress in time. There are a plethora of questions which may be raised about multiple choice test items :

- are they truly objective since human beings write test items?
- do they bias test taking/evaluation in that one kind of assessment technique is being used?
- how can test writers be certain that what is written is practical and relevant?
- with sometimes large standards of error of measurement within a test, how accurate is it to rank and compare pupils in test results

- what might the correlation be between test scores and future success at the work place and in society of an individual?
- how salient is it to include affective learnings in test taking? Attitudinal goals are equally important as compared to cognitive objectives, according to many educators.
- is measurable content picked for inclusion, such as facts, to the detriment of salient objectives such as caring and empathetic human beings?

Constructivism, as a psychology of learning, is quite different as compared to behaviourism. Instead of predetermined objectives for pupil attainment, consructivists emphasize that pupils are actively involved in learning whereby there is dynamic interaction among the teacher, the learning activity, and other pupils. Pupil learning by discovery is stressed rather than the teacher lecturing/ explaining to pupils. The teacher's role is to stimulate learner thinking in ongoing experiences in the curriculum. The purposes of the pupil are salient to foster; they have individual reasons for perceiving a need to achieve vital personal goals. Instead of answering a pupil's question directly in an ongoing lesson/unit of study, The teacher raises a related question to assist learners to think and come up with a relevant answer. The interests of pupils then are important considerations in the learning process. These interests propel learning and help pupils to put forth much effort in the classroom. Problem solving experiences is a good example in that a problem comes from learners. Learners develop a tentative answer or hypothesis to the problem. The hypothesis is tested in an authentic learning situation resulting in its acceptance, modification, or rejection. Problems are :

- identified by pupils with teacher assistance and clarification
- refined so they may be tested with the use of relevant experiences and activities

- new problems, identified by pupils, might well arise in these situations
- information sources to solve problems are used. The teacher always assists, encourages, and helps pupils in inquiry learning (Dewey, 1916).

How does the teacher assist in sequential pupil learning? A few examples might well indicate teacher involvement :

- instead of lecturing, explaining, and telling, the teacher asks ordered questions, leading the pupil to an answer.
- when pupils are reading to secure information, they may have problems with word recognition. Here, the teacher assists with the pupil using context clues, sounding out the word if phonetically spelled, looking for smaller words within the larger word, and/or dividing it into syllables.

References

Ahmad, Sajjad (2009), "Evolving a Framework for Teaching and Learning," *Edutracks*, 8 (9), 11-12.

Brady, Marion (2008), "Cover the Material or Teach Students to Think," *Educational Leadership*, 65 (5), 64-67.

Dewey, John (1916), *Democracy and Education*. Mew York: The Macmillan company.

Ediger, Marlow (2008), (The Old Order Amish and the Social Studies," *Viewpoints*, 38 (4), 13-16.

Ediger, Marlow (2009),"The Principal in the Teaching and Learning Process," *Education*, 129 (4), 574-578.

Ediger, Marlow, and D. Bhaskara Rao (2003), *Psychology and Curriculum*. New Delhi, India: Discovery Publishing House.

Teale, William H., and Linda B. Gambrell (2007), "Raising Urban Student's Literacy Achievement by Engaging in Authentic, Challenging Work," *The Reading Teacher*, 60 (8), 728-739.

15 CHAPTER

Testing, for What Purposes?

Pupils take a multiplicity of tests each school year. There needs to be a purpose for taking each test. Testing should not be done for its own sake, but it must serve a use and that being to provide the best curriculum possible for each learner. It is difficult to devise a high quality test. Tests must be valid in that they measure what it purports to measure. Thus, a test which states as its purpose to measure academic achievement must do so and not something else such as psychomotor skills. Tests taken by pupils should also be reliable in that a test taken again will yield the same/similar score for each learner.

Mandated Testing

Generally standardized tests are used when states mandate test taking. These tests have been tried out in pilot studies for validity and reliability. The statistical data from the pilot study is contained the Manual of the standardized test. Commercial companies have the needed funding and resources to devise, secure norms, and publish these tests. Local pupils test results may then be compared with the norm group in the Manual to indicate percentile standings. Grade equivalent norm scores may also be given.

In grades three through eight and an exit test must be taken by all pupils. If the grades three through eight mandated test is failed, then promotion to the next grade level will not be possible. Also the exit test taken in high school must be passed to ultimately receive a diploma in order to graduate. One test alone determines one's future to pass on to the next higher grade level. Measurement specialists do not perceive a single test as being adequate to be promoted. Additional data must be obtained other than from a single test to ascertain if a pupil is to be promoted, according to measurement specialists. There are additional questions which need to be raised about testing pupils. These questions include the following :

- How effective is any test in determining a pupil's future?
- What might be the correlation between a pupil's success in test results and the future work place? It is possible to work on these correlations.
- Are the test items truly relevant for pupils or are there other subject matter learnings and skills which need to be tested?
- Do mandated tests measure what is truly essential in life, such as good attitudes, caring for others, solving life's problems, as well as being a good citizen in society?
- Is test taking the personal style of the learner to reveal what has been learned? There are a plethora of means to indicate secured learnings such as making drawings, constructing items, and dramatizing, among others.

District wide tests may also be required for pupils to pass. District wide, as well as state mandated tests, generally contain multiple choice test items. With multiple choice tests, pupils choose the correct response from four distractors. Pupils react to a correct answer, but do not become active learners in composing an essay or a story. The test writers have determined which is the correct response with no latitude given for interpretation. Multiple choice test items may become too factual since one response or answer alone is sufficient. Clues for the correct answer, too, may be be given in the response which weakens multiple choice testing. Reasons given for multiple choice testing are the following :

- machine scoring may be used and many tests may be scored in a very short time.
- advocates believe they are objective with no bias involved in their scoring. The same key is used in scoring all tests taken on a particular grade level.
- the same time limits are given for test taking, regardless of the ability or learning style of the involved pupil. Pupils vary from each other in a plethora of ways and time limits do not adhere to providing for individual differences.
- the same directions apply to taking the standardized, multiple choice tests. Individual differences are not taken into consideration when directions for test taking are given.
- pupils having taken the test receive percentile results which spreads pupils out from high to low or vice versa. Each pupil's percentile may be compared with others having taken the same test.

In addition to mandated testing, pupils also take teacher written tests throughout the school year. Multiple choicer test items may then be in the offing. Each of the four distractors should match with the stem to be grammatically correct. They need to be of similar length so as not to provide clues as to which is the correct response. Multiple choice test items tend to measure recall of knowledge and do not stress high cognitive levels. In contrast, essay tests written by the teacher might well stress problem solving, critical and creative thinking purposes. They must then have as a purpose evaluation of higher levels of pupil thinking. Additional criteria to follow in writing essay tests include the following :

- the items should be delimited so that a reasonable amount of writing per item is emphasized. If answers are too lengthy, the responses may not deal with the needed subject matter. Thought questions with meaningful responses are wanted, not the amount of written ramblings. If too much delimitation is involved, one or two facts may be required, but this is the recall level only, and not higher levels of cognition. Vital factual information wanted from testing may be better appraised by using true/false, short answer, or matching test items.
- essay items must be written clearly in order to communicate what is wanted. Vague, hazy items may confuse the learner. Thus, in problem-solving, the problem must be clearly stated. The pupil needs to present an hypothesis, and then evaluate the hypothesis in terms of learner background information possessed, as well as iridepth thought. If the resulting information indicate, the pupil may revise the hypothesis.
- pupil's essays may be graded by giving a certain number of points for each of the stated problem given, the hypothesis, as well as the evaluation section of the hypothesis. Holistic procedures may also be used with a grade given for the entire essay item. Results then need to be assessed involving the pupil and the teacher in diagnosing and discussing. Selected evaluators stress the development and use of rubrics to objectify the grading process.

A few pointers must be mentioned pertaining to writing test items which stress recall of that which is truly relevant :

- there needs to be more items in column A as compared to column B when writing matching test items. Thus, the process of elimination may be minimized when pupils respond to a matching test. Single words or short phrases should be used in either column since it is too difficult for pupils to match lengthy sentences.

- short answer test items must have enough information within each sentence so that the learner knows what is wanted. The following is vague indeed :——— and ——— is the ——— of ———.

There are also *formative* evaluations to assist teachers to understand what pupils have left to learn in an ongoing unit of study. Here, test feedback provides the teacher with information on what needs emphasizing as the unit of study progresses. In contrast with formative is *summative* evaluation. Thus at the conclusion of a unit of study, the teacher reviews test results from pupils to ascertain how well the unit was taught and how much pupils learned. If the same unit is taught again, the teacher may make needed changes in objectives, learning opportunities, and assessment procedures when viewing pupil appraisal results from the summative evaluation. Additional tests used to appraise pupil achievement and progress include benchmarks. A teacher then may wish to test pupils to notice if target dates in teaching have been met by a certain time. The teacher has high expectations that pupils will attain optimally within a selected time framework.

Teacher Observation

Teacher observation of pupil achievement is rather continuous and he/she may observe at a given time when a learner needs assistance to move forward sequentially. Thus, when a pupil reveals at his/her desk that problems in "regrouping and renaming" in subtraction are in evidence, the teacher provides immediate help so that pupils attach meaning to and understand that concept. Here, the teacher may keep an anecdotal record of when and the kinds of help given to a pupil or a committee of learners. Teacher observation has been greatly minimized as an important way to appraise pupil achievement since :

- it can not be documented with numerical results as is true of standardized tests.
- it is considered subjective. However, all testing is subjective since human beings, for example, write standardized test items.
- it is not considered a part of the accountability movement.

Portfolios may also be considered to be a part of teacher observation to ascertain pupil achievement. They consist of a random sampling of pupil products such as written work, art samples, as well as digital photos of pupil's projects, among others. Each item in the portfolio is dated to notice sequential progress. The teacher assists the pupil to gather portfolio contents. Here, the teacher has ample opportunities to observe and help pupils achieve more optimally. During parent-teacher conferences, the portfolio contents may be viewed and discussed with the pupil involved. Portfolio contents may be rubric appraised to make the evaluation increasingly more objective. However, rubric results are not like machine scored multiple choice test results in securing a percentile or grade equivalent. But, a portfolio is an approach to connect with parents in working toward an improved curriculum for the learner.

IN CONCLUSION

What then are the purposes for testing? Mandated testing has a purposes to report pupil progress on the state level. The test scores for a district or entire state are there to make comparisons. How does a district or state fare as compared to others. Mandated tests are given also for purposes of promotion for pupils, presently, in grades three though eight and for an exit test on the high school level. Accountability of teachers, too, is a key purpose of mandated testing.

Teacher written tests attempt to measure pupil achievement within a unit of study or lesson. In addition to multiple choice test items, these may also be essay whereby pupils compose answers and can reveal strengths in problem solving.These problems are not like being in society and actually attempting to solve realistic, authentic dilemmas. Projects developed by pupils must be appraised separately since testing is definitely not involved here in a hands on approach in learning.

16

CHAPTER

Mandated Testing of Pupils Versus Constructivism

Mandated testing on selected grade levels for promotional purposes has proponents and opponents. Mandated testing provides data for use in tracking learner progress through the grades. It provides information on who graduates from high school. Mandated testing may provide information on how well pupils are achieving in school as well as pinpoint where sequential achievement has been lacking. A point of intervention is then emphasized to remedy or modify situations when a lull in progress appears.

Mandated testing has its negative side such as too many tests being administered in a given school year. Pupils might experience test anxiety and not do well in testing situations. Tests tend to evaluate pupils on factual information and not branch out to higher levels of cognition. They may not stress evaluating pupils on what is truly salient and difficult to measure. Mandates want precise data on pupils progress, not essay content whereby pupils have a greater voice in how to respond and organize ideas for writing.

Mandated testing then has advantages and disadvantages in indicating what pupils have learned.

Analyzing Mandated Testing

Mandated tests are given once a year to determine pupil promotion from one grade to the next. Measurement specialists state that high stakes testing such as this, should be determined by more than a single test. There are too many variables affecting a pupil's achievement with a one shot approach; these variables include physical health, the involved mental status of the learner, as well as variations in the quality of atmosphere surrounding the time of test taking, among others. Second, teachers feel forced to spend hours of time drilling pupils for taking the test. Drill is definitely not perceived to be a recommended way of involving pupils in learning, according to educational psychologists. Third, selected academic or curricular areas get slighted if reading, arithmetic, and science, only, are tested upon as in No Child Left Behind (NCLB) federal mandate. Balance in the curriculum emphasizes that social studies, art, music, and physical education, too, need to become a vital part of a well rounded set of experiences for pupils. Fourth, what is tested, gets taught. There are a plethora of news reports where this is true. School principals are under pressure to have pupils do well on tests for public relations endeavors. The results are published in local newspapers. No one desires to experience failure. Thus, teachers are coaxed to pressure pupils to achieve well on tests. Fifth, there are cases of dishonesty where pupils' answers have been changed or correct answers are given to pupils to up test scores, before they are sent to computers for scoring. Some have used the test directly in teaching, word for word as they appear on the mandated test. Sixth, a few educators say learning is cheapened when pupils are tested continuously on the content acquired. They indicate that learning should be its own reward. Seventh, selected reinforcement techniques such as giving prizes to pupils if they achieve well on tests may also be detrimental, according to some educators. Instead of learning for its own sake, pupils then work to achieve prizes for doing well.

Eighth, little thought has been given in ascertaining how valid and reliable the test content actually is. Is the subject-matter in mandated testing what pupils truly need to do well in school and in society? Ninth, teacher observation in terms of quality criteria is the best procedure to utilize in appraising pupils progress. Why? The teacher may almost immediately notice the kinds of assistance which need to be given learners as these observations are being made. Feedback from pupils within a specific learning situation provides teachers with information for ensuing objectives to emphasize in teaching and learning situations. These are ten salient reasons for not administering mandated tests to pupils (Ediger, 2008).

There are important reasons given for stressing mandated testing. Data from testing is used to track pupil achievement from one grade level to the next. Thus, teachers and school administrators may notice, on the monitor, sequential test scores of pupils and where progress was made as well as when a lack of progress occurred. Second, test scores communicate to parents how well their offspring is doing in school achievement. Objectivity is there with percentile ratings, for example, such as a child being on the fortieth percentile in mathematics. Parents, however, need to be informed as to the meaning of percentiles or other unit measures to ascertain pupil achievement such as stanines, or grade equivalents. Third objective measurements are used to convey information on learner progress. Instead of slogans on pupil achievement, there are precise measurements provided from test results. Thus, there is a "handle" on reporting learner achievement in numerical terms. Fourth, comparisons may be made between individuals and schools. Some believe then that to show realistic pupil progress, there need to be standards to indicate which schools are doing well and which need improvement, or even mandated changes in teachers and in school administrators for poor pupil performance. Fifth, forced changes need to be made in having teachers measure up and be held accountable. If pupils fail to achieve adequately, teachers are not performing well in teaching and learning. Thus, if a pupil is not promoted to the subsequent grade level due to a low test score, then this reflects upon the teacher. Other variables are left out of the equation such as poverty of the child. Sixth, parents should have the right for their offspring to attend a different school if test results show continuous failure of low performing schools. Thus, low performing schools can be identified through failure for their pupils to meet definite requirements. Seventh, the bully pulpit can be used by state and national officials to motivate pupil progress. Results from testing may always be criticized in terms of inadequate learner progress, regardless of improved achievement from the previous school year. Or, negative verbal statements made about what is deemed underperforming schools, the purpose being to "encourage" quality education. Eighth, financial rewards, in terms of merit pay, may be given to teachers of schools deemed to be high in achievement. It is relatively easy to look at test results as the indicator to ascertain which schools are doing well. Ninth, a nation losses out in world trade and prosperity if the educational system is not functioning well as measured by tests in making international comparisons. The school systems at the top in international comparisons will tend to do the best in economic competition. Tenth, pupils in schools who are close to making the mark for promotion may receive extra coaching since the average rate of doing well will be expanded in number, such as in adequate yearly progress (AYR). This may be detrimental to other pupils in the classroom (Campbell, 2007).

Constructivism in Philosophy of Education

Constructivism as a philosophy of education stresses that pupils assist in setting standards for achievement in ongoing lessons and units of study. They develop knowledge and skills and it is up to the teacher to motivate intrinsically, encourage, and promote learner achievement. Thus, the teacher, as well as pupils, provide learning opportunities within ongoing units of study. Pupils are challenged, not forced to learn what is perceived to be important, as well as learner purposes are involved to pursue and achieve. Perceptions change as new experiences are encountered; knowledge and skills, too, are then modified. Knowledge and skills are tentative and subject to change, they are not measurable. Critical and creative thinking as well as problem-solving are emphasized. The project method is also salient when pupils construct, make, and engage in hands on experiences in ongoing units of study. Pupils then arrive at their own unique truths through experiences. Through interaction with others and with materials of instruction, the pupil experiences and develops his/her own conclusions. Responsibility for learning resides within the learner, not the teacher nor in textbooks. Teachers facilitate and help pupils to achieve the latter's goals; support for learning comes from teachers, but definitely not in lecture form. Consructivist teachers are able to steer away from a deductive stance of teaching to one of assisting pupils to perceive their own values in learning. A relaxed learning environment which supports pupil thinking and in developing subsequent activities emphasizes a facilitating teacher who guides pupil ownership of ongoing experiences. Pupils then construct their own experiences, knowledge, and skills. They are active, not passive learners; learning by discovery is significant to constructivists thinking in education. Motivation to learn depends upon the confidence of the involved pupil in acquiring what is useful and has purpose (Mansilla and Gardner, 2008).

Vygotsky (1978) emphasized that pupils work in small groups so that ideas are shared and challenged; ideas then may "bounce off" the minds of individuals in a discussion setting. Learning occurs within a contextual authentic setting, not within a decontextualized lecture nor in testing situations. Assessment of learning is ongoing and continuous with teacher observation; assistance to learners is given as needed in helping pupils to experience what is necessary in learning.

Toward the other end of the continuum, with measurement philosophy of education, pupils reveal a definite amount of learning which can be shown in numerical terms. Either a pupil does/does not achieve an objective. There is no guesswork. E.L. Thorndike (1874-1949) expressed the heart of measurement philosophy. He stated that "Anything that exists, exists in some amount, and if it exists in some amount, it can be measured." The measurement movement then extended to all curriculum areas as well as in measuring attitudes and the affective domain. For example, in doing my doctoral dissertation in 1962-1963, We measured how student teachers affected pupil achievement in attitude development using the California Test of Personality. In this study, mathematics progress was measured using the mathematics section of the Iowa Test of Basic Skills. Thus, if anything exists such as art, music, and physical education achievement, these can be measured. Mathematics is as exact a science as any academic discipline and, no doubt, becomes the easist to measure to measure pupil growth and progress.

The measurement movement has certainly become strongly rooted in educational systems around the world as in the following :

- state and federal testing mandates.
- a voluntary system to measure a random sample of pupils in achievement such as the National Assessment of Educational Progress (NAEP).
- data driven systems of instruction.
- comparisons among nations from international test results.

A major weakness of measurement driven instruction is to ascertain in behavioral terms and prior to instruction what pupils are to learn. Is there that degree of certainty? Further problems in the selection of objectives, as well as in testing, include the following :

- might what is highly relevant be stated in precise measurable terms for pupil achievement, such as being a caring person as well as being a good citizen?
- factual knowledge of pupils is relatively easy to test; is too much emphasis then placed unon testing lower cognitive level objectives rather than critical and creative thinking, as well as problem solving?
- only what is measurable may be chosen as objectives for pupil attainment.
- may salient objectives be left out of the instructional arena when these are chosen prior to instruction?
- how much input should pupils have into curricular decisions within ongoing lessons and units of study such as in identifying a relevant problem area?

References

Campbell, Peter (2007), "Edison is the Symptom, NCLB is the Disease," *Phi Delta Kappan*, 438-443.

Ediger, Marlow (2008), "Mental Health and the Curriculum," *Journal of Instructional Psychclogy*, 35 (1), 38-42.

Mansilla, Veronica Bolz, and Howard Gardner (2008), "Disciplining the Mind," *Educational Leadership*, 65 (5),14-19.

Vygotsky, Len (1978), *Mind in Society*. Cambridge, Massachusettes: Harvard University Press.

17

CHAPTER

Evaluation of Pupil Achievement

Teachers need to be aware of using different methods of pupil evaluation at appropriate intervals. There are salient concepts which teachers need to be cognizant of in the evaluation process. Each evaluation technique has a purpose in its use as well as when it is to be utilized. Thus, evaluation has significant reasons for individual usage. The purpose of this paper will be to clarify meanings of each evaluation use.

Informal Evaluation Procedures

Somewhat continuously, the classroom teacher appraises pupils in ongoing activities throughout the school day. Teacher observation is then being utilized to notice what pupils have accomplished in a daily lesson plan as well as what should come subsequently in teaching and learning situations. The following activities provide points of intervention :

- when a word is not identified in reading
- when a pupil cannot think of a topic to write on
- when sequence in written work is lacking
- when the learner forgot what was to come next in an oral book report

- when a committee is not able to proceed in developing of an art project within a specific unit of instruction (Cuban, 2008).

Each of the above is an example of assistance to be given when carefully observing pupil progress. Teacher observation is ongoing and feedback from learners provide information on how well pupils are achieving. The teacher may wish to take notes on the types of help which needs to be given and how effective the assistance was for each classmate.

Anecdotal statements, as another evaluation technique, are recorded and dated written comments pertaining to observed pupil progress. The content here comes from teacher observations made such as the following anecdotal statements :

October 10. Alex volunteered too do an extra book report.

October 14. Bill is anxious to respond to questions in class, but his answers are very limited due to hurrying.

October 18. Maria has difficulties in thinking of ideas when writing poetry.

October 22. Norma bothers others who want to complete an assignment (See Ray, 2006).

With written comments, the teacher may be able to observe a pattern of behavior for each child. Comments written must be accurate and concise. They should assist the teacher in making better curricular decisions to help learners achieve more optimally.

Studying lesson plans which were used in teaching might also be classified as an informal evaluation approach. Thus, a small group of three to four teachers may evaluate the lesson plan of a committee member to ascertain its quality in the instructional arena. If need be, the lesson plan may be modified and tried out with a set of learners to notice its effects to optimize achievement. The following might have been modified :

- the sequence of learning activities
- provisions made for individual differences among pupils
- constructivism incorporated to help in harmonizing styles of learning (Ediger, 2006).

Teacher written tests, too, may be considered as being an informal means to ascertain achievement. These need to be valid and reliable. Clarity of writing is of utmost importance. Vagueness in test item writing does not assist pupils in revealing in what they know. Test items should be developmentally appropriate and on the understanding level of pupils. Multiple choice tests are frequently used here. There are rules for writing multiple choice test items such as :

- each response being plausible and of a similar length in order not to provide clues as to the correct answer
- each response together with the stem making for a grammatically correct sentence
- only one response being correct unless otherwise given in the test directions (Ediger, 2009).

True/false test items might also be written by the teacher. Guesswork is taken out of responding by having pupils indicate in writing what is incorrect in a test item.

Essay tests provide opportunities for pupils to construct their very own answers. Questions in an essay test need to be thought provoking and involve problem solving as well as be adequately delimited. The following then are two extremes to avoid in writing essay test items :

- What year was Jerusalem captured by the Crusaders? The answer requires a factual recall of a date and requires little in the line of thought and thinking.
- Write about the Crusades in world history. Volumes have been written on the Crusades and this topic is much too broad in scope for an essay test item (Ediger, 2008).

Adequately delimited test items might well be the following :

- Who were the Crusaders when they first organized in AD 1096?
- Why did people join the ranks in becoming a Crusader?

Essay tests reveal how well pupils write sentences which are grammatically correct as well as indicate spelling and handwriting skills. Evaluation should be based on correct information presented with the mechanical skills of writing graded separately. If pupils are ready and enough computers are available, they may use the word processor to construct answers. The latest in technology should be used in the curriculum. This, however, does not eliminate using longhand in written work. When supervising university student teachers in the public schools, several cooperating teachers stated they could not foresee the complete elimination of using paper and pen/pencil to communicate ideas. The writer advocates the use of word processors, and the latest in technology whenever feasible, relevant, and possible.

To objectify the evaluation process of essay responses, educators may recommend strongly that rubrics be used. Rubrics contain criterion to appraise essay responses. Generally, they are given on a five point scale. The criteria are then written out to serve as a guideline to appraise essay responses. The following is an example of a five point scale to use as a model to appraise responses from essay tests written in long hand :

Scale of five. The essay contains accurate statements given in a clear, logical manner. The ideas are presented sequentially.

Scale of four. The essay contains a few errors in information presented. But the information is presented in a logical and sequential manner.

Scale of three, the essay contains errors in information; logic and sequence are lacking in selected situations.

Scale of two. Errors in information distract from the essay as does logic in written sentences.

Scale one. The essay needs rewriting after the weaknesses have been pinpointed.

Evaluation of Achievement of Pupil Achievement in Unit Teaching

Formative evaluation is emphasized during the time a unit of study is taught. Here, the teacher wishes to find out what pupils have learned and there still is time to make changes before the unit culminates. Formative evaluation then may occur at any point, prior to its ending. Purposes for formal evaluation include the following :

- to ascertain what needs reteaching
- to determine what has been mastered by pupils
- to add new salient objectives for pupil attainment
- to make decisions on necessary review of selected concepts and generalizations
- to appraise the general achievement level of involved learners
- to make needed modifications and changes in the curriculum (Ediger, 2009).

Formative evaluation stresses assessment along the way, instead of at the end of a unit of study only. Teacher written tests may be used, in part, in formative evaluation such as multiple choice, true/false, essay, matching, and short answer tests. The teacher has a chance, in formative evaluation, to notice the effectiveness of his/her teaching. How successful was the teacher in the instructional arena involving unit teaching?

End of the unit appraisal pertains to *summative* evaluation. Here, the unit has been completed and the teacher desires to ascertain how much pupils have learned in achieving knowledge and skills objectives. Purposes inherent in summative evaluation are the following :

- have the instructional objectives been attained by pupils?

- what needs to be modified when teaching this unit the next time?
- are there other learning opportunities which might be more beneficial to learners than those used?
- should the order or sequence of activities be changed?
- did the evaluation techniques measure in a valid and reliable way?
- should a pretest be added so that progress may be measured using post-test minus pretest results? (Beckstead, 2008).

Standardized Testing

With the measurement movement being in vogue, many standardized rests are purchased by states to notice mandated achievement. Standardized tests indicate that each pupil has the same test items for the grade level being tested, the directions for test administration are the same for all, and the scoring key for computerized scoring is also the same. Generally, multiple choice test items are used since they may be scored with the same scoring key with exact, precise answers. Thus, on the print out, it is easy to notice the percentile rank of the pupil when compared to others having taken the same test. No allowances are made for language difficulties in speaking a different language than English. Nor are allowances made for slow learners, as well as those who are mentally retarded. Then, too, selected pupils need more time in test completion as compared to others. More variables result, if the teacher drills pupils on test taking procedures or uses a manual which assists pupils to secure higher test results.

There are further problems in that the test may not be valid for pupils if teachers have not had access to specific objectives directly related to items on the test, or if teachers did not carefully consider the objectives when teaching. The test may lack reliability if pilot studies were not run prior to standardization of the test. The Manual should provide specific results of validity and reliability. There are additional questions which arise pertaining to the use of standardized tests to measure pupil achievement :

- are the items relevant for pupils as citizens in society?
- does increasing test scores become the objective of schooling?
- do teachers and principals emphasize teaching to the test largely or only?
- does "what is on the test" count only or largely as teaching pupils?
- might the scope of the test be broadened to include such concepts as caring for others, having a positive attitude, and being a good citizen?
- should the mandated test also include questions pertaining to measuring achievement in the social studies, art, music, and physical education, in order to stress *balance* in the curriculum? (Wiggins and McTighe 2006).

Criterion Referenced Testing (CRT)

Whereas standardized testing stresses making comparisons among and between pupils' test results, CRTs emphasize the teacher teaching toward pupils achieving specific objectives of instruction. Comparisons in achievement then are not made among learners, but what is important is that all learners have ample opportunities to achieve the stated objectives. Some will take more time in doing so, as compared to others. There are no specific time limits here. The criterion in CRTs are the precisely stated objectives of instruction. Teachers need to realize the following in CRTS :

- it is clearly centered upon pupils achieving measurably stated objectives of instruction. Either, a pupil does/does not attain an objective as a result of instruction. For some advocates of CRTs, the objectives may be more open ended. In CRTs, a variety of learning opportunities may be implemented with the following standards in evidence.

- a variety of experiences to achieve objectives may be used here.
- proper sequence in choosing and implementing learning opportunities is salient.
- teacher feedback received of learner achievement due to the success or lack thereof in goal attainment.
- clarity in objectives so that the teacher knows if ordered objectives have been attained (Gill, 2008).

Benchmarks may be set up along the way as goals for pupils to attain by a selected time. The purposes here are to stay on track and have a specific time set to achieve a definite point on the continuum of learners progress. The question to be raised, "Are pupils making adequate progress in goal attainment?" Should pupils then have achieved more than where they are at the present time? The established benchmark will attempt to answer that question.

CONCLUSION

There are a plethora of beliefs pertaining to how pupil achievement should be evaluated. Teachers and school administrators must be well versed in each procedure in order to make quality decisions in curriculum improvement. Individual differences need to be provided for so each pupil may attain as optimally as possible.

REFERENCES

Beckstead, Larissa (2008), Scientific Journals: A Creative Assessment Tool," *Science and Children*, 46 (3), 22-26.

Cuban, Larry (2008), "The Perennial Reform: Fixing School Time," *Phi Delta Kappan*, 90 (4), 241-250.

Ediger, Marlow (2006), "Writing in the Mathematics Curriculum," *Journal of Instructional Psychology*, 33 (2), 120-123.

Ediger, Marlow (2009), "Scope in the Social Studies," *Edutracks*, 8 (6), 14-16.

Ediger, Marlow 2008), "The American High School," *College Student Journal*, 42(3), 814-817.

Ediger, Marlow (2009), "Reading Comprehension in the Science Curriculum," *Reading Improvement*, 46 (2), 78-80.

Gill, Sharon Ruth (2008), "The Comprehension Matrix: A Tool for Designing Comprehension Instruction," *The Reading Teacher*, 63 (2), 106-113.

Ray, Katie Wood (2006), "What Are You Thinking?" *Educational Leadership*, 64 (2), 58-62.

Wiggins, Grant, and Jay Me Tighe (2006), "Examining the Teaching Life," *Educational Leadership*, 63 (6), 26-30.

18

CHAPTER

Oral Communication in School Setting

Communicating orally is done very frequently. It is probably the most frequent means of communication in society. The school setting, too, should stress the importance of orally expressing ideas. Too frequently, the teacher does much of the communicating in a one way street of presenting subject matter. There needs to be more of interaction between the teacher and learners in using language to express facts, concepts, and generalizations, in an inductive manner. Students need to learn to use oral means of communication to become increasingly proficient in this method of conveying information in school and in society.

Learning Opportunities in Oral Communication

The teacher must capitalize on opportunities during the school day to advance students conveying information orally. In all curriculum areas, there are a plethora of chances to use discussions. To have pupils attach meaning to subject matter, learners need opportunities to critically examine content read. By assessing content read, pupils have opportunities to analyze subject matter. To analyze means to view separate areas of content read in terms of fact from opinion, fantasy from reality, as well as accurate from inaccurate content. Orally separating component parts and thinking critically about each assists the learner to move to higher levels of cognition. The teacher needs to be a change agent in leading students to do critical thinking. Active engagement is necessary in oral communication. Exciting discussions whereby each student participates must emphasize democracy as a way of life. Ideas presented by each person needs to be respected as worthwhile for a quality discussion. When watching TV newscasts, the writer is astounded at the lack of politeness when guest presenters from different political parties interrupt and disagree with each other in a very negative way. Certainly, there must be improved manners used in all walks of life in oral communication. Rudeness, intimidation, and crude behavior must be eliminated (Kieffer and Lesaux, 2007).

Second, pupils need to work in small groups or committees as well as in the previous large group discussions, advocated pupils work cooperatively in small groups. Interaction among members is salient. Ideas must circulate among small group members with each one participating and no one dominating. Rudeness and inconsiderate behavior need to be abolished in favor of respect and acceptance. Encouragement of member participation is a must! In literature circles pertaining to any academic discipline might well include the use of library books. Self selection of these books provide for individual differences in terms of reading levels and genre chosen. The topic must, however, relate directly to the unit of study being emphasized. As pupils interact, ideas presented bounce off the minds of presenters. Modified thinking might well result. Pupils need to view ideas from diverse perspectives (Vygotsky, 1934/1978).

The Zone of Proximal Development developed by Vygotsky, 1934/1978) reveals the importance of the teacher perceiving where the pupil is presently and comparing that with an ideal in achievement. This gap may be closed through scaffolding with quality learning experiences, carefully sequenced, and provided for students. It is significant to notice where a pupil is achieving at the present time as compared to a possible ideal and then thinking of eliminating/minimizing this gap (Ediger, 2006).

Third, pupils should reflect upon subject matter read and discussed orally. By reflecting, the pupil rehearses what was learned previously. Not only does the learner recall ideas, but also thinks about content acquired. This leads to a new synthesis. Ideas do not fall into separate categories, but become related. Related content is easier to remember as compared to a plethora of isolated subject matter. Challenging, new objectives need to be attained which are achievable. Feelings of belonging are salient to incorporate. If pupils feel that they belong and are accepted, an important need has been met. An emotionally, comfortable environment provides a good situation for coming up with new ideas when combining the old with the new learnings in terms of gleaning ideas (Keefe, 2007).

Fourth, metacognition stresses that teachers think about thinking to improve the curriculum for each pupil. To think about thinking, the teacher needs to look back to a previous lesson taught. There are questions that the teacher must ask of himself/herself such as the following :

- was the student ready for the new learning experience?
- were the learning activities carefully sequenced to obtain learner attention?
- was each activity engaging for the learner?
- did it appear that quality attitudes were a salient achieved objectives of the lesson?
- did students ask important questions during the lesson presentation?
- if off task behavior occurred, what might have been the cause(s)?

By thinking about the previous lesson taught, the teacher may be able to come up with important answers. These answers are usable to improve the quality of teaching for future lessons to be implemented. Metacognition strategies, properly used, might well assist in curriculum improvement (Ediger and Rao, 2007).

Fifth, multiple intelligences theory emphasizes that pupils have different abilities and talents. Thus, pupils individually may possess the following intelligences individually, among others :

- verbal intelligence as in reading and writing
- logical reasoning as in mathematics
- musical as in writing lyrics and putting the words to music

  intrapersonal whereby the learner attains more optimally in studying by the self
- interpersonal in which the student does well in cooperative endeavors
- bodily kinesthetic whereby the learner excels in tasks involving eye/hand coordination and physical prowess (Gardner, 1993).

For each of the above intelligences, it is important to be able to communicate well orally. The listener must be able to hear and listen to the communicator. Only then, can the listener respond to what was said. Both the communicator and the listener have salient responsibilities to have meaningful communication.

References

Ediger, Marlow (2006), "Scaffolding and the Reading Curriculum," *Iowa Educational Leadership*, 8 (4), 24-26.

Ediger, Marlow, and D. Bhaskara Rao (2007), *Reading Curriculum and Instruction*. New Delhi, India: Discovery Publishing House.

Gardner, Howard (1993), *Multiple Intelligences : Theory Into Practice*. New York: Basic Books.

Keefe, James W., "What is Personalization?" *Phi Delta Kappan*, 89 (3), 217-213.

Kieffer, Michael J., and Nonie K. Lesaux (2007), "Breaking Down Words to Build Meaning: Morphology, Vocabulary, and Reading Comprehension in the Urban Classroom," *The Reading* Teacher, 61 (2), 134-145.

19

CHAPTER

Listening with a Purpose in School Setting

There are a plethora of opportunities to secure information through listening in school and in society. Individuals need to make a conscious effort to listen carefully to a message which goes from the sender to the receiver. Good listeners have strategies available in listening to ideas presented and the purpose of any strategy is to comprehend. Specific reasons for listening may vary. Listening is a very salient way of learning. It is one method, among others. This paper will discuss specific purposes and goals for listening to ongoing messages.

Developing Good Listening Habits

A lack of background information may truly hinder the ability to comprehend content through listening. Readiness is important in the listening process. Thus, the student needs to possess necessary facts, concepts, and or generalizations to understand what a speaker is communicating. Wide reading is needed to possess readiness for listening to many presentations. Even then, the background information may not be adequate due to many possible topics to discuss and listen to. The listener may monitor if comprehension is occurring by rehearsing content to the self which is acquired through listening. Hazy or omitted content might well provide a basis for asking questions and seeking answers (Ediger, 2008).

Being curious and wanting to increase knowledge and skills helps in learning content through listening. Turning off on a speaker whose topic does not interest the listener may rob the person of growth in the language arts. The listener must desire to pay attention to ideas expressed and not focus on mannerisms and other factors which may distract. A *deliberate* attempt to listen carefully is salient indeed. Sometimes, individuals have closed minds and do not wish to receive ides expressed by a speaker. Students need to accept diversity of ideas; otherwise increased knowledge and abilities do not come about. Being open minded is very important if new subject matter is to accrue. Listeners must realize that one's thinking occurs more rapidly than ideas can be expressed. At the same time, listeners need to focus on the importance of listening to different facets or kinds of subject-matter (Ediger, 2007).

Metacognition and Listening

With metacognition strategies, the listener thinks about thinking. He/she thinks about what was communicated and reflects upon these ideas. The listener then evaluates what can be done to improve listening habits. He/she might well realize that selected facets of knowledge and skills are missing. Opportunities then present itself to minimize these gaps. Problem solving is involved when the learner identifies questions which require answers. Information is then located to fill the gaps. By evaluating the quality of listening, the student becomes increasingly aware of areas which need improvement. A synthesis of ideas occurs between the subject matter already possessed and the newly accrued content (Dymock, 2007).

Then too, metacognition may emphasize thoughts pertaining to higher levels of cognition than the recall level of ideas acquired. Analytic thinking may be stressed in listening to evaluate. Here, the learner separates ideas into component parts. Relevant from the irrelevant may be separated in order to solve a problem; problem solving is always important in school and in society. Or, in project methods of instruction, skills needed to construct a model, to be made, are separated from those unnecessary for project completion. In a discussion pertaining to an ongoing unit of study, students may think critically about the central idea pertaining to what was read. Subordinate content is separated from the main idea. Students may then reflect upon on the salient versus that which was not central to achieving an objective. This might mean revising one's thinking. Conclusions realized are tentative and subject to change (Wallace, 2007).

There are a variety of purposes for listening. The learner may listen to an ongoing classroom discussion to secure information. Listening to subject-matter presented by the teacher might even emphasize, as a purpose, to doing better on a formative or summative test. Or in a music class, the student listens carefully to classical music as a purpose. Sheer enjoyment of listening to the lyrics and the accompanying melody might be a salient goal.

Oral communication provides numerous worthwhile opportunities to listen and learn. The following listening activities might then be in the offing :

- book reports given with appropriate guidelines followed
- peer discussion groups and peer teaching
- transmediation experiences when translating from one media to the next, such as from written work to artistic drawings, involving speaking and listening activities
- debates pertaining to issues in current events
- poster contents, such as provisions made for alternative forms of energy, whereby students explain

meaningfully to peers about content provided therein with careful observations made of audience listening habits

- oral reading to peers with quality listening being assessed (Barton, 2006).

There are then a plethora of listening activities available to students. The list could readily be expanded to include listening to and evaluating multimedia presentations, including power point, DVDs, and video tapes, among others. Each presentation needs to be integrated with an ongoing lesson or unit of study. Students must conscientiously decide to focus on the listening task at hand. Comprehension of facts, concepts, ideas, and generalizations should result. These need to become an inherent part of the listener whereby he/she assesses the worth of the content by adding information and/or by thinking creatively. Creative thinking stresses bringing in novel, unique ideas. Originality of thought is salient in creative thinking (Mohanty, 2008).

Quality thinking and listening is involved when learners make the following connections :

- connecting the content being considered to the self. The ideas being presented are then related to the student's own life experiences
- connecting the textual content to other texts which have been read or considered. Perceiving the relationship of ideas is important
- connecting the considered content with the world, such as current happenings on the local, state, national, and international levels (Ediger, 2007).

Each of the above expands and enriches the thinking of learners. Listening and speaking experiences abound. Criteria for listening need to be developed and then each student needs to be evaluated in terms of improving over previous achievement in listening. Through listening, learners may accept, refute, or modify previously held beliefs. They may also place ideas in appropriate categories as well as perceive patterns in knowledge. Comparisons may be made of new and previously held subject matter. Then too, creatively, the listener might develop novel, unique ideas. Detecting bias while listening to a speaker/presenter is also salient. The tone of voice, enunciation, stress, and pitch of words might well influence a listener. In addition, the listener needs to watch for inaccurate statements as well as content dealing with fantasy versus reality (Cai, 2008).

There need to be periodic class discussions on what makes for quality listening habits. Appropriate listening skills need to be practiced and feedback obtained as to meeting each standard. Appraisal results need to be secured to notice if learners are more successful in listening as compared to prior evaluations. If, for example, a developmental appropriate poem is read aloud to students, can they retell its major elements? Are there happenings in the classroom environment which hinder effective listening? These might include classroom noise, distractions, unpleasant temperature readings, and discipline problems, among others. Excessive drill and routines in learning activities hinder good listening in the classroom. Boredom may then set in (Krishnamoorthy, 2007).

Having pupils listen for the central idea of a recording, developmentally appropriate, may challenge many students. The teacher needs to model and discuss the meaning of a main idea. Several learning activities are necessary to assist learners to understand and determine a main idea. Thus from the contents, students need to state in one sentence the expressed main idea. After a reasonable amount of time, students may be asked to write their individual perceived main idea. From written work at their desk to writing the main idea on a white board makes it possible for viewers to evaluate each statement. Perhaps, five or six pupils may each write their main idea on the whiteboard. Pupils seated at their desks might well compare their main idea with that of a presenter. This is indeed a thinking experience. It is difficult to write in one sentence subject-matter contained in the recording. During the discussion, there will be numerous disagreements on which is the main idea. Students will discuss the following, among others, from the written statements of their central idea contained in the recording :

- does additional information need to be incorporated? Students may then say why additional information needs to be added to more thoroughly reflect the central idea.
- should information be deleted from a written statement due to its lack of importance? Debates and discussions should be welcomed in the thinking situation involving reflection, metacognition, and learner efficacy.
- might ideas be combined to form a central idea? Sometimes, ideas being presented for the central idea are too similar to list separately.

The writer observed and participated in the above named experience at Bethel College (North Newton, Ks) during the Fall Quarter 1950-1951 school year. It was indeed challenging to participate on the college level and he has observed it being used when supervising university student teachers.

Ideally, all pupils need to participate in the discussion/ debate. No one should dominate. Respect for diversity of ideas needs to be encouraged. Rudeness and ridicule do not belong in any ongoing activity. Pupils tend to refrain from participation if ideas are not wanted. Too frequently, a clique may dominate the discussion, but it must not be that way! Democracy as a way of life must be stressed here.

To make it very personal in a listening set of experiences, students may be asked to list what was listened to in the home setting during the after school hours until bed time. The day of the assignment my be specific as well as the deadline for the activity should also be a certain time such as

May 6. During class time, learners might compare their listings. Items such as the following may accrue :

- listening to a blue jay sing
- hearing the sounds of cars pass by
- enjoying the sounds of children at play
- participating in a home discussion
- listening to a musical recording by George Friedrich Handel
- hearing particular sounds of shoppers while shopping in a neighboring convenience store.

Lists may be combined on the white board with no overlapping items to show the number of different sounds which students listened to. Additional different sounds may be brainstormed. This may be an exciting experience for students as they think of sounds not listed!

The teacher may use ongoing classroom activities to promote quality listening. Thus, during story time when the teacher reads aloud to students, he/she may ask questions of listeners pertaining to content read. These can be stimulating questions which which encourage higher level of cognition when responding. For a change of activity, listeners may draw a picture of their favorite character, setting, plot, or happening.

A favourite activity of students is to have learners place their heads on the desk top and not view the sound being made by a peer. The listener then guesses the source of the sound. Selected sounds made may be quite obvious to listeners; however, there will always be very unique sounds for students to guess their source.

REFERENCES

Barton, Paul E, (2006), Needed : Higher Standards for Accountability," *Educational Leadership*, 64 (3), 28-31.

Cai, Mingshui (2008), "Transactional Theory and the Study of Multicultural Literature," *Language Arts* 85, (3), 212-220.

Dymock, Susan (2007), "Comprehension Strategy Instruction: Teaching Narrative Text Structure Awareness," *The Reading Teacher,* 61 (2), 161-167.

Ediger, Marlow (2008). "The American High School," *College Student Journal,* 42 (3), 814-817.

Ediger, Marlow (2007), "Teacher Observation to Assess Student Achievement," *Journal of Instructional Psychology,* 34 (3), 137-139.

Ediger, Marlow (2007),"The Substitute Teacher in Reading instruction", *The SubJournal*, 8 (2), 67-73.

Krishnamoorthy, R. (2007), Select Personal and Institutional Variables in Relation to Receptivity to Change Among Arts and Science College Teachers, Chapter Two. Ph D thesis, Madurai Kamarj University, India.

Mohanty, Jagannath (2008), "Multimedia Approaches in Learning," *Edutracks*, 7(11), 19-20.

Wallace, Christopher (2007), "Vocabulary; The Key to Teaching English Language Learners to Read," *Reading Improvement,* 44 (4), 189-193.

20

CHAPTER

For an Effective Reading Programme

An effective program of reading instruction must meet the needs of pupils individually. Pupils in a classroom differ from each other on present reading achievement levels. They also come to the classroom with diverse abilities, interests, and attitudes toward reading and literacy in general. Thus, the reading teacher must consider a plethora of factors when assisting learners in the teaching of literacy. What makes for a quality program of instruction?

Quality in the Reading Curriculum

Teachers and supervisors need to plan a reading program which motivates pupils. The content should contain literature which is of interest to learners. Pupils may then be observed in being actively engaged in reading. The teacher must provide readiness experiences prior to pupils being involved in the reading process. Readiness emphasizes motivated pupils who benefit from the ensuing activity. Stimulating questions pertaining to the new content needs to be in the offing. If basals are used, the illustrations therein provide readiness ideas for a discussion of related subject matter. From the discussion, pupils raise questions which they would like to have answered. Reading the ensuing content might well provide those answers. Prior to the reading experience, pupils need to be introduced to possible new words to be read. These may be highlighted by being shown on the computer screen or by using the overhead projector. The teacher needs to be certain that pupils can identify these words while reading and understand their contextual meaning. With interesting methods used to identify questions as well as present the new words in context, pupils should feel motivated to read the ensuing lesson. Exciting discussions tend to follow (Ediger and Rao, 2007).

Second, adopted reading programmes should be based on a firm research and theoretical base. Outdated ideas and opinions need to be discarded. Meaning theory of reading instruction should be emphasized. Learners need to understand content in literary selections. Meaning attached to the setting, characterization, plot, irony, and theme make for eager learners wanting to do more reading of narrative content. Expository subject-matter can make for equal enthusiasm in its reading. Answering questions pertaining to different facets of content increases interest. Children love to speculate on literary elements pertaining to "What if," questions. They like to scaffold ideas based on stimulating points of view presented. Indepth meanings might then well accrue (Ediger, 2007).

A favourable classroom climate needs to be promoted to help learners achieve more optimally. The reasons why teachers like to control students instead of managing them are :

- They are socialized to believe or are instructed that the marks of a good teacher is to have control over the class.
- The amount of control teachers have in the class is often seen by the administrator as a measure of the quality of a teacher.
- They are afraid of losing control if students have increased autonomy.

- They fear that students with with less control will not want to learn what the teacher wants to teach (Bindhu, 2008).

Teachers and school administrators need to promote a classroom climate which is conduce to pupil learning. A relaxed, studious atmosphere must prevail. Pupils should like school and the different curriculum areas taught. If pupils do not care for education and schooling, reasons for this occurring must be diagnosed. Pleasant school surroundings need to replace that which is negative. The next standard might, in part, help to make for needed change in the curriculum.

Third, pupils should choose reading materials from a wide variety of fascinating library books. Thus, from a variety of topics and genres on display in the classroom, the learner may choose an interesting library book to read. Pupils need to have ample opportunities to make choices and decisions, from among alternatives. The choices stress choosing a library book, among others, to read sequentially, during time devoted to individualized reading. The teacher needs to assist pupils to choose sequential library books for silent reading who initially cannot settle down to select and read a library book. The teacher needs to observe which pupils are/are not actively engaged in individualized reading. Self selection of reading materials encourages skills in decision making and promotes pupil responsibility in making choices (See McConachie, et. al., 2006).

Creativity is a key goal in literacy. The pupil needs encouragement to read creatively. Unique interpretations of what has been read is salient. Individual or collective creativity in responses are important. Originality of interpretation may be shown through :

- art products such as drawings, pencil sketching, mural development, and water color products
- construction experiences including making models, paper mache' items, and puppets

- poetry writing such as haiku, tankas, quatrains, limericks, and free verse
- dramatic experiences including pantomimes, and creative dramatizations (Tiedt, 1982).

Novel works should always be encouraged from and through a variety of reading experiences. They may well be means of indicating comprehension from reading and discussions.

Different genres must be available for pupil selection of reading materials. Pupils possess unique interests in subject-matter content. Attractive books, readily available, should be checked out with ease. These books may be introduced by the teacher and/or the school librarian. Introduced books need to be shown to students with a stimulating, short introduction read aloud. Selected library books may also be read aloud to students during story time. Voice inflection with proper stress, enunciation, and pitch assist in drawing learner attention to the contents during the read aloud.

The teacher as well as with student involvement need to develop attractive bulletin boards involving one or more new library books. The display needs to capture student attention. Book jackets of newly purchased library books, pictures of authors, and illustrations pertaining to these library books must be in the offing. Introduction of each subsequent bulletin board display should assist learners to do more reading of quality literature. A concerted effort should be made to encourage more learner reading. If library books are read sequentially, this will assist pupils to become increasingly proficient in reading. Reading needs to be an enjoyable activity. Of all skills possessed by the writer, reading would come first in importance. This does not minimize different academic areas since much reading is required to learn and achieve in each academic discipline. The act of reading is a skill and that skill is used to gather information for course work, the work place as well as for enjoyment. Each academic area also has its own requirements such as experimentation in the science curriculum. Reading of subject-matter, for example, relates well to doing experiments and further indepth studies in science. Reading is equally salient in doing word problems in mathematics and attaching meaning to mathematical symbols. In the social sciences, pupils need to become proficient in reading primary and secondary sources of information.

A quality library book reading program will assist pupils to do more reading be it expository, narrative, and/or creative content such as poetry. What is read needs to be assessed. This goes beyond securing ideas literally from the selection(s) read. Critical reading stresses separating facts from opinions, fantasy from reality, as well as accurate from inaccurate content. Concepts and generalizations might then be realized from the synthesis.

Aesthetic reading stresses that pupils individually react and interpret content, based on previous experiences. Cai (2008) wrote the following :

> Aesthetic reading is personal, but is not simply identifying with characters or expressing personal likes and dislikes about the story, as is frequently misinterpreted. Aesthetic reading is a rather complicated process that includes evocation and responses.

Cai goes on to quote Rosenblatt (1982) pertaining to aesthetic reading:

> In aesthetic reading, we respond to the very story or poem we are evoking during the transaction with the text. In order to shape the work, we draw on our past reservoir of past experiences with people and the world, our past inner linkage of words and things, our past encounters with spoken or written texts. We listen to the sound of words in the inner ear; we lend our sensations, our emotions, our sense of being alive, to the new experience which we feel, corresponds to the to the text. We participate in the story, we identify with characters, we share their conflicts and their feelings. At the same time, there is a stream of responses being generalized. There may be a sense of pleasure in our own creative activity,

an awareness of pleasant or awkward sound and movement in the words, a feeling of approval or disapproval of the characters and their behaviour.

Critical reading may follow with analyzing and value judgments made. Standards are used in making the evaluative statements. Students need to demonstrate individual reading successes in the following ways :

- using teacher observation in terms of recommended criteria
- evaluating the self in individual and cooperative learning endeavors
- results from teacher written tests such as essay and multiple choice items
- assessing art, dramatic, and written products of learners directly related to literacy content read (Ediger, 2008).

References

Bindhu, T.S. (2008), "Dynamics of Classroom Management," *Edutracks*, 7 (10), 15-17. Published in India.

Cai, Mingshui (2008), "Transactional Theory and the Study of Multicultural Literature," *Language Arts*, 85 (3), 215.

Ediger, Marlow, and D. Bhaskara Rao (2007), *Reading Curriculum and Instruction*. New Delhi, India : Discovery Publishing House.

Ediger, Marlow (2007), "The Substitute Teacher in Reading Instruction, *SubJournal*, 8 (2), 67-73.

Ediger, Marlow (2008), "Philosophy of Testing, Measurement, and Evaluation," *Edutracks*, 7 (10), 25-26.

McConachie, *et al.* (2006), "Task, Text, and Talk, Literacy for All Subjects," *Educational Leadership*, 64 (2), 8-15.

Rosenblatt, Louise (1982), "The Literary Transaction: Evocation and Response," *Theory into Practice*, 21 (4), 268-277.

Tiedt, Iris M. (1982), *The Language Arts Handbook*. Englewood Cliffs, New Jersey; Prentice-Hall, Inc.

21

CHAPTER

Seven Criteria for an Effective Classroom Environment

There are a plethora of variables which affect pupils in the classroom. These might involve the obvious such as uncomfortable temperature readings a well as the following :

- small group work as compared to individual activities.
- use of measurably stated objectives versus constructivism as, psychologies of learning.
- a very quiet environment compared to business like surroundings.
- zero tolerance in discipline as compared to pupil/ teacher planning of rules for classroom conduct.
- teacher directed learning activities compared to a learner centered approach.
- lecture/explanations versus critical and creative thinking as well as problem solving experiences.
- traditional seating arrangements in rows and columns as compared to flexible room arrangements (Ediger, 2005).

In each of the above asterisked items, committees need to work on solutions to these issues in order to resolve the dilemmas. Committees individually need to report to the total group to seek input. Eventually, several approaches may be used such as individual as well as group endeavors to meet needs of learners. Teachers and school administrators benefit when diverse ideas are presented and research is done to gather necessary information in formulating conclusions, following much deliberation. Beyond these items listed above, an appropriate related classroom environment must be in the offing in teaching and learning situations. This environment facilitates pupils achievement of relevant objectives of instruction.

Favourable Learning Environments

Proactive strategies need to be in the offing to minimize/ eliminate negative behavior such as harassing others. Being harassed hinders pupil achievement and progress. Relevant rules discussed with pupils and adequate supervision should assist in identifying cases of harassment. These cases need to be handled in a way in which pupils can perceive the harm inflicted on others when harassment is in evidence. Not only does the victim feel hurt, but the perpetrator tries to get away with what he/she feels is manly or womanly. But, in all reality, it is humiliating to both. Inwardly, the perpetrator sees the consequences of his/her acts. No one likes to be called unwanted names, be mimicked with unbecoming language, being hurt physically, and or experience emotional damage. Pupils experiencing harassment should have a place to report grievances. A counselor, well versed in this area, should respond immediately to cases of harassment. The victim needs to be listened to carefully, and the perpetrator needs immediate counseling to modify and change behavior (Ahmad, 2009).

Second, classroom rules need to assist in avoiding misbehavior of pupils. Misbehavior might well consist of bothering others to hinder learning, including bursts of anger and talking back to the teacher. Politeness toward others, involving both teachers and learners, is essential for any classroom to perform and function well. A community of learners emphasizes cooperation in developing an environment conducive to optimal pupil achievement in academic, social, and psychomotor skills (Ediger, 2009).

Third, pupils from different cultural groups must be accepted as individuals having much worth. No one desires to be excluded, but wishes to possess feelings of belonging. Recent immigrants from abroad should not be shunned, but rather integrated so they can reveal talents possessed through their native art, dress, music, language, dances, as well as foods eaten. Sharing of culture broadens educational horizons of classmates and enriches lives. There are diverse ways of meeting personal needs and human culture reveals these differences (Sapon-Shevin, 2008). For example when eating with bedouins in the Middle East, the writer observed smacking of lips is good in order to show excellence in tasty foods eaten, but in the US, of course, it violates folkways and morays.

Fourth, pupils need to have ample opportunities to work in cooperative learning situations. They need rules to follow such as each pupil in the committee being actively involved, ideas circulating among members in the group, politeness and consideration for others being stressed, and clarity of content being expressed by pupils. Classroom environments improve when criteria are used to foster positive human relationships. Each participant in learning must be valued and quality human values must pervade instruction (Petress, 2006).

Fifth, pupils individually need to feel important for personal accomplishments be it in school or in society. For example, if a slow learner improves in achieving, this needs to be rewarded with praise for actual accomplishments. There are numerous rewards given pupils for achieving outside the school setting, such as 4H, Boys and Girl Scouts, Boys and Girls Clubs, and FFA, among others, which provide opportunities for pupil recognition in the school setting.

Esteem needs must be met of learners. These assist pupils to develop motivational feelings to realize higher levels of attainment. The classroom teacher must assist pupils to feel motivation to reach out, grow, and accomplish. Talents of learners individually need to be adequately provided for in the school setting. Receiving recognition for attained goals is significant for anyone in the classroom, teachers included. There is certainly nothing wrong with a teacher saying what he/she accomplished in school and in society. Teacher achievement is a model for others to emulate (Ediger, 2008).

Sixth, the feeling dimension is too frequently omitted in teaching and learning situations. Perhaps, much of this is due to the testing movement whereby scores on mandated tests receive the most attention in a school day. These tests focus on academic achievement. Cognitive objectives are then emphasized highly and attitudinal (affective) ends receive short schrift. Advocates of Emotional IQs stress the importance of the feeling dimension in school and at the work place. Thus, a person may have high subject matter knowledge, but get along very poorly with others. Individuals are dismissed from various jobs because of having poor attitudes toward work, the work place, and toward those employed there. Rude, inconsiderate behaviors are the downfall of these individuals. Learning activities which are satisfying and perceived worthwhile helps pupils to develop well emotionally (Booker, 2008).

Seventh, pupils must understand what is taught and not merely memorize subject-matter for a test. Meaning attached to ongoing experiences helps learners to achieve sequentially. Subsequent activities are built upon previously acquired knowledge and skills. The ensuing then becomes comprehensible and readiness for learning is then in evidence. Interests, too, are fostered if meaning is there.

References

Ahmad, Saijad (2009), "Evolving a Framework for Teaching and Learning," *Edutracks*, 8 (9),11-12. Published in India.

Booker, Keonya (2008), "The Role of Instructors and Peers in Establishing a Classsroom Community" *Journal of Instructional Psychology*, 35(1), 12-16.

Ediger, Marlow (2005), *Quality School Education*. New Delhi India: Discovery Publishing House.

Ediger, Marlow (2009), "Technical Education, the Work Place, and the Student," *American Technical Education Journal* (ATEA), 36 (2), 18-19.

Ediger, Marlow (2008), "Current Events in the Social Studies," *Social Studies Review*, 47 (2), 58-60.

Petress, Ken (2006), "An Operational Definition of Class Participation," *College Student Journal*, 40 (4), 821-823.

Sapon-Shevin, Mara (2008), "Learning in an Inclusive Classroom," *Educational Leadership*, 66 (1), 49-53.

22 CHAPTER

Supervising the Student Teacher Schools

The student teacher being supervised in the public school soon becomes a full time, licensed teacher. Student teaching is perceived to be the cap stone or final course in undergraduate preparation before entering the profession of being a teacher. It carries much responsibility for the cooperating teacher and the university supervisor in assisting the student to emphasize quality in helping pupils to achieve as optimally as possible. The university supervisor and the cooperating teacher must work together to provide a quality student teaching experience. Student teachers need to be adequately prepared to meet obligations of becoming a true professional (Ediger, 2007b).

Preparing Student Teachers

Prior to the student teaching experience, the pre-service teacher has been engaged in general education course work, methods of teaching classes, seminars, field experiences, as well as observation and participation in classrooms. These experiences have assisted the prospective student teacher to gain knowledge, skill, and understandings pertaining to teaching and learning situations. The university supervisor will now have the responsibility of assisting the student teacher to integrate what has been previously acquired in teaching pupils in the public school classroom. The supervisor will also need to clarify expectations for the student teaching experience. What will the supervisor expect of the student teacher during the time allotted to this final activity prior to becoming a full time licensed teacher? The following need to be clarified with the student teacher :

- lesson plans development for each lesson taught
- a unit to be developed for unit teaching
- a seating chart of pupils in the classroom
- grouping of pupils for instruction
- conference expectations of the university supervisor
- evaluation considerations for student teaching
- working responsibly with the cooperating teacher.

Evaluation of Student Teaching

Prior to each observational visit, the university supervisor needs to clarify the objectives to be emphasized in teaching pupils with the student teacher. Clarity of meaning is important in what will be emphasized in teaching and learning situations. The learning activities on the daily lesson plan need to match up with each intended objective. The evaluation techniques listed assist in ascertaining what pupils have learned from the lesson taught.

During the time the lesson is taught, the university supervisor needs to record salient information on teaching and learning being stressed by the student teacher. This needs to be done in a manner which does not distract the student teacher from doing a good job of teaching. Developing a good self concept is a must for the student teacher.

It is important to notice if pupils are actively engaged in the lesson. Interest in learning is a powerful factor in educational psychology. If selected pupils did not appear to be interested, what might be suggested during conference time with the student teacher to aid in pupil lesson engagement? A notice needs be filled out so that the student teacher may work on recorded deficiencies (Ritchhart and Perkins, 2008).

Second, pupils need to understand content taught. If subject-matter is not meaningful, pupils will reveal this lack of understanding during discussions, tests taken, or in future learnings emphasized. Learning is sequential and what is not understood presently will hinder subsequent progress. Hurrying to teach new subject matter will not suffice when the present lacks meaning for the pupil. Readiness for learning accrues when the previously presented knowledge and skills possess meaning. Whatever is taught must be taught well. Meaningful subject matter provides sequence for ensuing knowledge and skills to be attained (Burke, 2005).

Third, pupils must perceive purpose in learning. Thus, reasons need to be in evidence for achieving selected ideas. If purpose is lacking, pupils will lack perceiving relevance in the objectives to be attained. The student teacher may assist pupils inductively or deductively to perceive purpose in learning. The writer when supervising pre-service teachers has noticed how pupil attitudes change in a positive direction when they are assisted in noticing the relevance of acquiring new knowledge and skills. University student teachers need guidance in assisting pupils to perceive purpose in learning. Sometimes, simply stating in a few words why the ensuing content is important to be learned is adequate!

Fourth, university students are generally used to hearing complex ideas in coursework taken on campus. They may need considerable assistance in communicating ideas on the understanding level of the public school pupil. Teaching involves effective communication in either an inductive or deductive approach. Subject-matter needs to be presented in a manner that is understandable to learners. To ascertain if directions, for example, are understood for doing a lesson, a pupil may be asked to repeat what was said in his/her very own words. After having given an assignment, the student teacher my observe if the ensuing work is done properly. Adequate leeway must be given, too, to have pupils do creative work whereby novel ideas are presented and appreciated. Originality is salient in writing creative poetry, stories, and plays, as well as in art work (Ediger, 2007a).

Fifth, the student teacher needs to provide for individual differences in the classroom. Pupils differ from each other in diverse ways. Thus, some pupils like to study and learn in small groups; others prefer individual activities to pursue. Selected pupils prefer quiet activities such as reading and writing experiences while others prefer to work on projects where physical movement and motion are involved. Additional differences among pupil choices are the following

- assigned class work as compared to making choices from among alternatives
- a quiet classroom versus movement and motion of learners engaging in learning
- being seated in rows and columns versus a flexible arrangement of classroom furniture for learning
- teacher supervision of learning as compared to self monitoring of progress.

Each pupil has a preference for specific kinds of learning activities, such as those listed above. But still, each pupil needs a combination of activities such as working by the self as well as with others. Both are salient in that individuals need to do learning activities by the self as well as work together with others in class. Later at the work place, individuals will do tasks by the self as well as with others. Student teachers need to observe and appraise pupil progress in either situation (Ediger, 2006).

Positive attitudes of teachers toward their profession will shape their students into becoming good citizens. As teacher education programmes are the most significant methods for developing positive attitudes toward teaching and the teaching profession, the assessment of attitudes of student teachers over time helps to evaluate the effectiveness of experiences provided, changes in training and procedures, or the general progress of program implementation. The results can help to improve programme design and implementation, daily procedures of pre-service teacher education programs, and support services.

One of the challenges we see facing teacher education at the present time, is our need to respond to the tension in our pre-service education programs between development of individuals as professionals and the demands of professional programs that must ensure teaching competency (Devanandan, 2008).

Supervision of Reading Instruction

Reading, as one curriculum area, receives much attention in the school setting. The student teacher needs assistance to guide pupils in sequential and remedial work. Young readers need guidance in beginning reading instruction such as in using the Big Book approach. Here, a class of five to seven children are taught using a big book, clearly visible to all in the group. Readiness for the ensuing reading activity is promoted through a discussion of the related illustrations in the big book. The teacher reads aloud to the pupils, pointing to each word being read. Pupils follow along by viewing the printed script. In the next read aloud, both the teacher and pupils are involved. This may be repeated as often as necessary. Pupils leam to identify the new words by sight. There is no embarrassment of pupils who cannot otherwise recognize unknown words.

The university supervisor assists the student teacher in bringing in new approaches in teaching which aid in providing for individual differences in the classroom. Additional approaches in reading instruction to assist the student teacher in providing for individual differences include the following:

- using the basal reader more creatively by stressing new ideas along with those in the manual. Thus, the basal should not be used in a stultifying manner, but rather emphasize teaching suggestions which assist pupils to achieve more optimally.
- implementing individualized reading by having pupils select and read silently sequential library books of their very own choosing during a designated time in class.
- emphasizing literature circles whereby peers choose and read a library book involving a stimulating discussion of the contents. Here, peers help each other in reading within a cooperative learning situation (Clarke and Holwadel, 2007).

The university supervisor and cooperating teacher help students to grow, develop, and achieve during the student teaching experience.

References

Burke, Karen (2005), "Teacher Certification Exams: What Are the Predictors of Success," *College Student Journal*, 39 (4), 784-793.

Clarke, Lane W. and Jennifer Holwadel, "Help! What is Wrong with These Literature Circles and How Do We Fix Them?" *The Reading Teacher*, 61 (1), 20-31.

Devanandan, K. V. (2008), Attitudinal Changes of Student Teachers in Colleges of Education Affiliated to Mahatma Ghandi University, Kottayam. Ph D thesis, Aiagappa University, Karaikudi, India.

Ediger, Marlow (2006), "Scaffolding and the Reading Curriculum," *Iowa Educational Leadership*, 8 (4), 24-26.

Ediger, Marlow (2007a), "Meaning in Reading In Reading Instruction," *Reading Improvement*, 44 (4), 217-220.

Ediger, Marlow (2007b), "Teacher Observation to Evaluate Achievement," *Journal of Instructional Psychology*, 34 (3), 137-139.

Ritchhart, Ron, and David Perkins (2008), "Making Thinking Visible," *Educational Leadership*, 65 (5), 57-63.

23 CHAPTER

Teaching the Gifted Child

The gifted child needs challenging objectives to attain, learning opportunities which motivate, and evaluation procedures which truly assess what has been learned in a valid and reliable way. He/she cannot be left alone without teacher assistance, but rather needs to experience guidance and direction to feel challenge in the curriculum.

Gifted learners are those who achieve at a faster rate as compared to average ability students. They retain learnings longer and posses increased motivation to learn. Gifted students tend to be curious and have an inward desire to learn. Gifted student motivation to learn may wane if they receive little teacher attention. Being recognized for contributions made is salient for the gifted as well as for others. Thus, it is important for the gifted to have esteem needs met.

Learning Opportunities and the Gifted Learner

Which kinds of learning opportunities should be provided to assist the gifted to achieve more optimally? Encouragement, acceptance, and support are three concepts relevant in teaching the gifted. There are activities for the gifted to pursue which have wide transfer values in school and in society. Problem-solving is one. Here, the teacher must assist the learner to identify a relevant problem in context. This is a problem about which the student is curious. Curiosity stimulates learning and achieving. An adequately delimited problem contains a perplexing question which takes time and deliberation to answer. The problem has an hypothesis and requires considerable information for testing. Information comes from a variety of reference sources including the internet, excursions, consultants, textbooks, library/trade books, peers, among others. The hypothesis is then modified or changed if need be. When assisting the gifted in problem selection, developing hypotheses, and testing each hypothesis, there is heavy student involvement (Dewey, 1916). Since that time, there have been numerous advocates of using a problem solving approach in teaching and learning situations.

Closely related to problem solving is the project method (Wahlquist, 1942). The project method was initially developed by William Heard Kilpatrick (1871-1965), late professor of Columbia University in New York City. Various educators presently recommend strongly its use in the instructional arena. Dr. Kilpatrick emphasized four flexible steps in doing projects. The first step was to determine a purpose or reason for doing the project. It is valuable to perceive purpose in doing anything, rather than aimlessly working in class on something which does not make sense and has little value. After, the purpose has been established, the student carefully plans how to do the project. Planning carefully is different than haphazardly pursuing a plan. This is followed by carrying out the project to its completion. Next, criteria for assessment are developed and used for evaluation standards. These criteria represent what is considered quality work. Problem solving and the project method are both methods of being active learners rather than being passive recipients of knowledge. Activity methods of instruction are then in evidence. Problem solving and project methods allow for a wide variation of interests and multiple intelligences which are highly suitable then for gifted learners.

There are educators who advocate the basics in the curriculum for student acquisition. The late William Chandler Bagley (1874-1946) was an early advocate of emphasizing the basics in subject matter learning for students. The academics were very important to Bagley. He opposed activity centered procedures such as problem solving and project methods of instruction used exclusively in teaching and learning situations. Rather, he believed in students acquiring essential subject matter. This approach stresses the importance of students achieving essential subject matter (Ediger and Rao, 2004).

Basic subject-matter can be identified for gifted learners. Thus, the content complexity in achievement levels would go well beyond that of average achievers. When using graded levels of textbooks in mathematics, for example, gifted students might then reach sequentially more complex objectives by using graded texts well beyond the present grade level of the involved learner. The sky would be the limit of progress which could be made in mathematics. The use of a carefully chosen basal might well be one way of having the gifted achieve at higher levels in subject matter goal attainment. Being interested in the gifted child's welfare and progress are necessary in providing for individual differences. The home and school must work together for the good of the gifted learner. Face to face parent/teacher conferences may be supplemented with e-mail and telephone messages to plan effective strategies of instruction (Ediger, 2007).

Many/most gifted students will be college bound and need a challenging curriculum to prepare for professional studies in higher education. Talent must not be wasted, but motivated and encouraged! Kennedy and Tipps (1991) indicate the following cluster of characteristics for gifted and talented students :

- accelerated pace of learning
- sees relationships and readily grasps big ideas

- higher levels of thinking : applications and analysis easily accomplished
- verbal fluency; large vocabulary, expresses well orally and in writing
- extraordinary amount of information
- intuition, easily leaps from problem to solution
- tolerates ambiguity
- achievement and potential have close fit
- masters advanced concepts in field of interest.

Teachers need to study children to notice the latter's abilities, talents, and interests. The above named traits might well be of assistance to teachers in the assessment process. Each student needs to experience quality in terms of challenging objectives, learning opportunities, and evaluation techniques to appraise progress. With much ability, gifted learners need to make optimal progress in school and in society. Future leaders, professionals, and achievers are inherent in any class of gifted students. Now is the time for teachers to provide the kinds and types of experiences which will guide sequential progress for each gifted learner.

Well trained and educated teachers possessing self-efficacy should be in the classroom teaching gifted students. These are teachers who have and possess a strong feeling of capability to motivate children in teaching and learning situations. They have shown good models of success. Hoy and Miskel (2005) summarized the following pertaining to different theories which make for success in achievement.

Goal setting theory suggests that people work hard when :

- They have realistic, specific, and challenging goals
- They are committed to the goals
- They receive feedback about progress toward the goals.

Attribution theory suggests that people work hard when they believe that causes for success are :

- Internal-due to ability and effort
- Not fixed-effort, for example can vary from one situation to another
- Controllable - causes can be controlled by hard work, using proper strategy, etc.

Equity theory suggests that people work hard when they have been treated fairly and

- They have been given the rewards they deserve
- The rewards have been allocated fairly
- They have been treated with respect and courtesy

Expectancy theory suggests that people work hard when

- They believe their efforts will improve performance
- Good performance will be noticed and rewarded
- The rewards are valued.

Viewing the above summarized theories, there are selected concepts which are salient such as challenging, commitment, feedback, progress, ability, effort, hard work, rewards, and respect. These make for quality teaching and learning situations. The following are omitted even though they may be observed in a school setting: routine, memorization, punishment, and drudgery. With the latter four concepts, motivation, energy levels, and creativity go downhill. Individuals, including the gifted, do need to be rewarded for effort and achievement.

IN CONCLUSION

Gifted students need to be identified and adequate provision made for their progress. Children with special gifts or talents have a remarkable degree of general ability and/or extra-ordinary specific abilities. Furthermore, they display advanced creativity and are highly motivated to achieve in the areas of their ability and talent. They will often persevere on a problem far beyond the point where other children lose interest or give up. Such children in the elementary grades usually handle subject matter easily because of their capacity to use language and understand abstract relationships. Their work is sometimes "over the top"—very advanced for their age (Parker 2001).

REFERENCES

Dewey, John (1916), *Democracy and Education*. New York: The Macmillan Company.

Ediger, Marlow (2007), "Motivational Efforts to Improve the Curriculum," *Iowa Educational Leadership*, 9 (2), 19-21.

Ediger, Marlow and D. Bhaskara Rao (2004), *Elementary Curriculum Improvement*. New Delhi, India: Discovery Publishing House.

Hoy, Wayne K., and Cecil G. Miskel (2005), *Educational Administration, Theory, Research, and Practice*. Seventh Edition. New York: Me Graw-Hill, Inc., Chapter Four.

Kennedy, Leonard M., and Steve Tipps (1991), *Guiding Children's Learning of Mathematics*. Sixth Edition. Belmont, California: Wadsworth Publishing Company.

Parker, Walter C. (2001), *Social Studies in Elementary Education. Eleventh Edition*. Upper Saddle River, New Jersey, pp. 46-47.

Wahlquist, John T. (1942), *Philosophy of American Education* New York: The Ronald Press Company.

The American High School Experience

There have been numerous criticisms of the American High school and yet it continues to flourish in society. Various recommendations over the years have been made for its improvement. What are major complaints pertaining to the American High School? Which remedies might help for their renewal?

Criticisms of the High School and Remediation

When reading educational journal articles and teacher education textbooks on the American High School, certain statements appear which appear to be rather consistent.

High school students say that courses taken are boring ad lack purpose. Then a problem exists in how to make subject matter interesting as well as meet needs of students. Dropout rates of students remain relatively high. Are methods of teaching used a dilemma in securing learner interests? If so, then the methods of teaching used need to be modified. There are a variety of methods which might capture learner attention. These include :

- problem- solving methods as well as project development

- increased use of discussions
- committee work and peer mediated discussions
- inductive/deductive alternatives as methods of instruction
- large group, small groups, and individualized instruction in sequence
- block of time approaches (Ediger and Rao, 2006).

In addition to changes in methodology used in teaching to avoid student boredom, modifications may be made in course work taken. Thus, a greater emphasis may be placed upon electives chosen by the student. The interests of the learner is stressed here. He/she may choose an increasing number of courses to be taken which are perceived to be more relevant than some of the prescribed classes. Electives might well include technical and vocational classes. There will be students who will go directly to a work place following high school graduation and adequate provision must be made for all students. Also, selected students will be attending a technical school/college following high school graduation. Regardless of the path taken in high school course work, each student needs to be prepared for higher education, technical education, or work place endeavors following graduation. On line education courses has aided in making provisions for individual differences among learners (Klecker, 2007).

In addition to elective courses, subject matter content may also be altered for student learning by :

- emphasizing an integrated curriculum, such as history and literature being correlated. For example, when a unit on the Civil War is taught, students may also study literature written in Civil War times.
- stressing individual endeavours by encouraging students to pursue an independent study, directly related to the ongoing unit being studied. Thus, for example, the student may choose to do an indepth study of The Underground Railroad prior to and

during the Civil War. The means of revealing what was learned may be shown through a variety of media including written and oral presentations with art work being a part of the indepth study. A peer committee might also work together to develop an indepth study.

- the class as a whole making a bound volume pertaining to an ongoing unit of study, whereby each student does quality work in developing a selection for the book. The means, whether by written or art work, is up to the student. The presenting of his/her ideas needs to come from the learner,
- setting up learning stations developed by students with teacher assistance. Each station has four tasks on a card from which students individually may make subsequent choices for completion. Each task pinpoints objectives to be achieved in an ongoing unit of study.
- using library books/internet sources to secure information directly related to the ongoing unit of study. Students may then respond to teacher questions covering content read such as on the Civil War. The chosen content read may be used in place of or in addition to the basal textbook.
- doing oral reports, in terms of recommended standards, whereby the student chooses a specific topic of the engaged unit to report upon. Instead of an individual report, students may also choose classmates to work on a cooperative endeavor (Ediger, 2006).

To evaluate learner achievement, a variety of valid and reliable means must be used. Teacher observation, in terms of recommended criteria, may be used continuously. These criteria might well include the following :

- sequential progress made by the learner over previous endeavors
- interest shown by the student in ongoing lessons and units of study

- questions raised by the student pertaining to what was not understood so that meaningful learning is achieved
- students learning to monitor their own progress
- reflecting on previous facts, concepts, and generalizations emphasized in the curriculum
- development of increased self efficacy in learning whereby the student develops confidence and self esteem
- achievement in working harmoniously with others (See Guskey *et al.*, 2006).

Additional methods to be used in appraising student progress include responding to teacher written test items. Multiple choice test items containing a stem and four rational distractors as well as true/false test items may be used to notice student achievement and progress. The guessing factor for the latter may be minimized by having a student cross out what is false and writing in the correct response.

Mandated tests should be used along with other procedures of evaluation to notice what remains to be learned by the student. Mandated tests must be supplemented with other approaches of assessment, such as those listed above. All tests must be used for diagnostic purposes, What has been diagnosed in terms of errors made by the student might well require re-teaching or remedial activities. Additionally, portfolios are recommended as evaluation devices and need to contain the following :

- a random sampling of written products of the learner such as poems and stories, reports, summaries, outlines, and plays.
- art products directly related to completed lessons and units of studies
- photos of competed construction projects
- videos of formal and creative dramatics experiences, oral as well as book reports and committee work experiences (Brown, 2006).

IN CONCLUSION

There are a plethora of steps which may be taken to alleviate student boredom on the secondary level. Student input into curriculum development may assist learners to perceive purpose in learning. A relevant curriculum is needed to prepare students for higher education, technical school, as well as the work place.

REFERENCES

Brown, Dennis (2006), "Motivating Effort on Standardized Tests," *Iowa Educational Leadership*, 8 (4), 14-19.

Marlow Ediger (2006), "Administration of Schools," College Student Journal, 40 (4), (346- 851).

Ediger, Marlow, and D. Bhaskara Rao (2006), *Quality School Education*. New Delhi, India: Discovery Publishing House.

Guskey, Thomas R., *et al.* (2006), Literacy Assessment, New Zealand Style," *Educational Leadership*, 64 (2), 74-79.

Klecker, Beverly M. (2007), The Impact of Formative Feedback of Student Learning in an Online Classroom," *Journal of Instructional Psychology*, 34 (3), 161-165.

Additional Reading

Amala, P. A. and Anupama, P., authors and Digumarti Bhaskara Rao, editor (2004). *History of Education.* New Delhi : Discovery Publishing House. ISBN 81-7141-860-0.

Appala Naidu, P.Ch., author and Digumarti Bhaskara Rao, editor (2007). *Student Feedback Methods.* New Delhi : Discovery Publishing House.

Bhaskara Rao, Digumarti (1994). *Scientific Aptitude.* New Delhi : Ashish Publishing House. ISBN 81-7024-658-X.

Bhaskara Rao, Digumarti (1995). *Animal Kingdom.* New Delhi : Discovery Publishing House. ISBN 81-7141-274-2.

Bhaskara Rao, Digumarti (1995). *Batracology.* New Delhi : Discovery Publishing House. ISBN 81-7141-279-3.

Bhaskara Rao, Digumarti (1997). *Scientific Attitude.* New Delhi : Discovery Publishing House. ISBN 81-7141-381-1.

Bhaskara Rao, Digumarti (1996). *Scientific Attitude vis-à-vis Scientific Aptitude.* New Delhi : Discovery Publishing House. ISBN 81-7141-308-0.

Bhaskara Rao, Digumarti (2004). *Scientific Attitude, Scientific Aptitude and Achievement.* New Delhi : Discovery Publishing House. ISBN 81-7141-781-7.

Bhaskara Rao, Digumarti (2004). *Educational Administration.* New Delhi : Discovery Publishing House. ISBN 81-7141-842-2.

Bhaskara Rao, Digumarti (2004). *Issues in School Education.* New Delhi : Discovery Publishing House. ISBN 81-8356-025-3.

Bhaskara Rao, Digumarti, editor (1996). *Encyclopaedia of Education For All,* 5 volumes. New Delhi : APH Publishing Corporation. ISBN 81-7024-759-4 (set).

Vol. I *Education For All : The World Conference.* ISBN 81-7024-760-8

Vol. II *Education For All : The EPA-9 Summit.* ISBN 81-7024-761-6

Vol. II *Education For All : Quality Education For All*. ISBN 81-7024-762-6.

Vol. IV *Education For All : Planning and Monitoring*. ISBN 81-7024-763-4.

Vol. V *Education For All : The Indian Scenario*. ISBN 81-7024-764-0.

Bhaskara Rao, Digumarti, editor (1999). *International Encyclopaedia of AIDS*, 11 volumes. New Delhi: Discovery Publishing House. ISBN 81-7141-522-6 (set).

Vol. 1 *Introduction to HIV/AIDS*. ISBN 81-7141-523-7.

Vol. 2 *HIV/AIDS – Issues and Challenges*, 2 parts. ISBN 81-7141-524-5.

Vol. 3 *HIV/AIDS – Socio Economic Realities*. ISBN 81-7141-524-3.

Vol. 4 *HIV/AIDS – Law Ethics and Human Rights*, 2 parts. ISBN 81-7141-526-1.

Vol. 5 *AIDS and NGOs*. ISBN 81-7141-527-X.

Vol. 6 *AIDS and Home Care*. ISBN 81-7141-528-8.

Vol. 7 *STD Case Management*. ISBN 81-7141-529-6.

Vol. 8 *HIV/AIDS Prevention and Care – Teaching Modules for Nurses and Midwives*. ISBN 81-7141-530-X.

Vol. 9 *HIV Prevention Education for Educational Institutions*. ISBN 81-7141-531-8.

Vol.10 *Instructional Modules for AIDS Education*. ISBN 81-7141-532-6.

Vol.11 *School Health Education to prevent AIDS and STD – A Package for Curriculum Planners*. ISBN 81-7141-533-4.

Bhaskara Rao, Digumarti, editor (2000). *International Encyclopaedia of Human Rights*, 7 volumes in 13 parts. New Delhi : Discovery Publishing House. ISBN 81-7141-567-9 (set).

Vol. 1 *International Instruments of Human Rights*, 2 parts. ISBN 81-7141-569-4.

Vol. 2 *Regional Instruments of Human Rights*. ISBN 81-7141-604-7.

Vol. 3 *Human Rights and the United Nations*, 2 parts. ISBN 81-7141-605-5.

Vol. 4 *Fact Files of Human Rights*, 3 parts. ISBN 81-7141-606-3.

Vol. 5 *Study Stories of Human Rights*, 3 parts. ISBN 81-7141-607-3.

Vol. 6 *International Meetings on Human Rights*, 2 parts. ISBN 81-714-608-X.

Vol. 7 *Professional Training in Human Rights*. ISBN 81-7141-609-8.

Bhaskara Rao, Digumarti, editor (2000). *International Encyclopaedia of Science and Technology Education*, 11 volumes. New Delhi : Discovery Publishing House. ISBN 81-7141-548-2 (set).

Vol. 1 *Science and Technology Education.* ISBN 81-7141-568-7.

Vol. 2 *Science Education in Developing Countries.* ISBN 81-7141-569-9.

Vol. 3 *Organizational Structure of Science.* ISBN 81-7141-570-9.

Vol. 4 *Science Education in Asia and the Pacific.* ISBN 81-7141-571-7

Vol. 5 *Science and Technology Education For All.* ISBN 81-7141-572-5.

Vol. 6 *Values, Ethics, Talent and Girls in Science and Technology Education.* ISBN 81-7141-573-3.

Vol. 7 *Popularization of Science and Technology Education.* ISBN 81-7141-574-1.

Vol. 8 *Science, Power and Society.* ISBN 81-7141- 575-X.

Vol. 9 *Information Technology.* ISBN 81-7141-576-8.

Vol.10 *Teacher Training in Science and Technology Education.* ISBN 81-7142-577-6.

Vol.11 *Teacher Training in Science and Technology : A Curriculum Framework.* ISBN 81-7141-578-4.

Bhaskara Rao, Digumarti, editor (2000). *Education For All : Achieving the Goal*, 3 volumes. New Delhi : APH Publishing Corporation. ISBN 81-7648-152-1 (set).

Vol. I *The Global Consensus.* ISBN 81-7648-155-6.

Vol. II *Mid-Decade Review Reports of Regional Seminars.* ISBN 81-7648-154-8.

Vol. III *Issues and Trends.* ISBN 81-7648-155-6.

Bhaskara Rao, Digumarti, editor (2004). *International Encyclopaedia of Learning to Live Together*, 4 volumes. New Delhi : Discovery Publishing House. ISBN 81-7141-848-1.

Vol. 1 *International Conference on Learning to Live Together.*

Vol. 2 *Globalization and Living Together.*

Vol. 3 *Curriculum for Learning to Live Together.*

Vol. 4 *Science Education for the Contemporary Society* .

Bhaskara Rao, Digumarti, editor (2005). *Encyclopaedia of Education For All*, 3 volumes. New Delhi : Discovery Publishing House. ISBN 81-7141-647-0 (set).

Bhaskara Rao, Digumarti, editor (2007). *Encyclopaedia of Teacher Education*, 4 volumes. New Delhi : Discovery Publishing House. ISBN 81-8356-306-6 (set).

Bhaskara Rao, Digumarti, editor (2007). *Encyclopaedia of Edeucation for Living Together*, 4 volumes. New Delhi : Discovery Publishing House. ISBN 81-7141-848-1 (set).

Bhaskara Rao, Digumarti, editor (1996). *National Policy on Education*, 2 volumes. New Delhi: Anmol Publications Pvt. Ltd. ISBN 81-7488-323-1.

Bhaskara Rao, Digumarti, editor (1996). *Global Perceptions on Peace Education*, 3 volumes. New Delhi : Discovery Publishing House. ISBN 81-7141-319-6.

Bhaskara Rao, Digumarti, editor (1997). *Education for the 21st Century.* New Delhi : Discovery Publishing House. ISBN 81-7141-389-7.

Bhaskara Rao, Digumarti, editor (1997). *Reflections on Scientific Attitude.* New Delhi : Discovery Publishing House. ISBN 81-7141-319-6.

Bhaskara Rao, Digumarti, editor (1997). *Success Story of a Primary Education Project.* New Delhi : APH Publishing Corporation. ISBN 81-7024-850-7.

Bhaskara Rao, Digumarti, editor (1997). *World Food Summit.* New Delhi : Discovery Publishing House. ISBN 81-7141-386-2.

Bhaskara Rao, Digumarti, editor (1997). *Care the Child*, 2 volumes. New Delhi: Discovery Publishing House. ISBN 81-7141-394-3.

Bhaskara Rao, Digumarti, editor (1998). *Earth Summit*, 2 volumes. New Delhi : Discovery Publishing House. ISBN 81-7141-435-4.

Bhaskara Rao, Digumarti, editor (1998). *Adolescence Education.* New Delhi : Discovery Publishing House. ISBN 81-7141-432-X.

Bhaskara Rao, Digumarti, editor (1998). *Community and School Nutrition Education.* New Delhi : Discovery Publishing House. ISBN 81-7141-435-4.

Bhaskara Rao, Digumarti, editor (1998). *District Primary Education Programme.* New Delhi: Discovery Publishing House. ISBN 81-7141-396-X.

Bhaskara Rao, Digumarti, editor (1998). *National Policy on Education : Towards an Enlightened and Humane Society.* New Delhi : Discovery Publishing House. ISBN 81-7141-426-5.

Bhaskara Rao, Digumarti, editor (1998). *Reforming School Education.* New Delhi : Discovery Publishing House. ISBN 81-7141-403-6.

Bhaskara Rao, Digumarti, editor (1998). *Teacher Education in India.* New Delhi : Discovery Publishing House. ISBN 81-7141-406-0.

Bhaskara Rao, Digumarti, editor (1998). *World Summit for Social Development.* New Delhi : Discovery Publishing House. ISBN 81-7141-420-6.

Bhaskara Rao, Digumarti, editor (2001). *Nuclear Materials : Issues and Concerns*, 2 volumes. New Delhi : Discovery Publishing House. ISBN 81-7141-611-X.

Bhaskara Rao, Digumarti, editor (2001). *Distance Education in Different Countries.* New Delhi : APH Publishing Corporation. ISBN 81-7648-229-3.

Bhaskara Rao, Digumarti, editor (2001). *Decentralised Management of Education : Management of Education in Panchayati Raj and Municipal Bodies.* New Delhi : Discovery Publishing House. ISBN 81-7141-617-9.

Bhaskara Rao, Digumarti, editor (2001). *Electrochemistry for Environmental Protection.* New Delhi: Discovery Publishing House. ISBN 81-7141-619-5.

Bhaskara Rao, Digumarti, editor (2001). *Global Educational Studies.* New Delhi : Discovery Publishing House. ISBN 81-7141-616-0

Bhaskara Rao, Digumarti, editor (2001). *Global Synthesis of Educational Assessment.* New Delhi : Discovery Publishing House. ISBN 81-7141-613-6.

Bhaskara Rao, Digumarti, editor (2001). *Jomtein Decade of Education.* New Delhi : Discovery Publishing House. ISBN 81-7141-618-7.

Bhaskara Rao, Digumarti, editor (2001). *World Conference on Education for All.* New Delhi: APH Publishing Corporation. ISBN 81-7141-274-9.

Bhaskara Rao, Digumarti, editor (2001). *World Conference on Higher Education.* New Delhi : Discovery Publishing House. ISBN 81-7141-610-1.

Bhaskara Rao, Digumarti, editor (2001). *World Conference on Science.* New Delhi : Discovery Publishing House. ISBN 81-7141-612-8.

Bhaskara Rao, Digumarti, editor (2003). *Inspiring Experiences in Teacher Education.* New Delhi : Discovery Publishing House. ISBN 81-7141-656-X.

Bhaskara Rao, Digumarti, editor (2003). *International Studies in Education*, 3 volumes. New Delhi : Discovery Publishing House. ISBN 81-7141-647-0.

Bhaskara Rao, Digumarti, editor (2003). *Military Conversion : Impact on Science and Technology.* New Delhi : Discovery Publishing House. ISBN 81-7141-578-4.

Bhaskara Rao, Digumarti, editor (2003). *United Nations Millennium Summit.* New Delhi : Discovery Publishing House. ISBN 81-7141-632-2.

Bhaskara Rao, Digumarti, editor (2003). *World Assembly on Aging.* New Delhi : Discovery Publishing House. ISBN 81-7141-637-3.

Bhaskara Rao, Digumarti, editor (2003). *World Conference on Human Rights.* New Delhi: Discovery Publishing House. ISBN 81-7141-661-6.

Bhaskara Rao, Digumarti, editor (2003). *World Education Forum.* New Delhi: Discovery Publishing House. ISBN 81-7141-639-X.

Bhaskara Rao, Digumarti, editor (2003). *Education, Employment and Human Resource Development.* New Delhi : Discovery Publishing House. ISBN 81-7141- 681-0.

Bhaskara Rao, Digumarti, editor (2003). *Successful Schooling.* New Delhi : Discovery Publishing House. ISBN 81-7141-677-2.

Bhaskara Rao, Digumarti, editor (2003). *European Education and Teachers.* New Delhi: Discovery Publishing House. ISBN 81-7141-702-7.

Bhaskara Rao, Digumarti, editor (2003). *Teachers in a Changing World.* New Delhi : Discovery Publishing House. ISBN 81-7141-694-2.

Bhaskara Rao, Digumarti, editor (2004). *International Guidelines on Open and Distance Teacher Education.* New Delhi: Discovery Publishing House. ISBN 81-7141-777-9.

Bhaskara Rao, Digumarti, editor (2004). *Adult Learning in the 21st Century.* New Delhi: Discovery Publishing House. ISBN 81-7141-797-3.

Bhaskara Rao, Digumarti, editor (2004). *Educational Practices : Research and Recommendations.* New Delhi: Discovery Publishing House. ISBN 81-7141-835-X.

Bhaskara Rao, Digumarti, editor (2004). *General Secondary Education In the 21st Century.* New Delhi: Discovery Publishing House.

Bhaskara Rao, Digumarti, editor (2004). *Reforming Secondary Education.* New Delhi: Discovery Publishing House. ISBN 81-7141-843-0.

Bhaskara Rao, Digumarti, editor (2004). *Human Rights Education.* New Delhi : Discovery Publishing House. ISBN 81-7141-882-1.

Bhaskara Rao, Digumarti, editor (2004). *United Nations Decade for Human Rights Education.* New Delhi : Discovery Publishing House. ISBN 81-7141- 887-2.

Bhaskara Rao, Digumarti, editor (2004). *Technical and Vocational Education and Training in the 21st Century.* New Delhi : Discovery Publishing House. ISBN 81-7141- 984-4.

Bhaskara Rao, Digumarti, editor (2005). *Encyclopaedia of Education For All,* 5 volumes. New Delhi : Discovery Publishing House.

Bhaskara Rao, Digumarti and B.S.V. Dutt, editors (2003). *Education : Programmes and Policies.* New Delhi : APH Publishing Corporation. ISBN 81-7648-470-9.

Bhaskara Rao, Digumarti, C.A.P. Swamy and B.S.V. Dutt (1997). *Self-Evaluation in Student Teaching.* New Delhi : Discovery Publishing House. ISBN 81-7141-374-9.

Bhaskara Rao, Digumarti and C. D. Swarna Lattha, editors (2006). *Encyclopaedia of Biotechnology*, 5 volumes. New Delhi : Discovery Publishing House. ISBN 81-8356-168-3 (set).

Bhaskara Rao, Digumarti, C. Sridevi and K. Vijaya (1995). *Achievement in Social Studies*. New Delhi: Discovery Publishing House. ISBN 81-7141-281-5.

Bhaskara Rao, Digumarti and D. Naresh Kumar (2004). *School Teacher Effectiveness*. New Delhi : Discovery Publishing House. ISBN 81-7141-

Bhaskara Rao, Digumarti and D. Sridhar (2002). *Job Satisfaction of School Teachers*. New Delhi : Discovery Publishing House. ISBN 81-7141-652-7.

Bhaskara Rao, Digumarti and Digumarti Pushpa Latha, editors (1998). *International Encyclopaedia of Women*, 5 volumes. New Delhi : Discovery Publishing House. ISBN 81-7141-410-9 (set).

Vol. 1 *Status of World's Women*. ISBN 81-7141- 494-X

Vol. 2 *Women, Education and Empowerment*. ISBN 81-7141-498-1.

Vol. 3 *Women Challenges and Advancement*. ISBN 81-7141-497-4.

Vol. 4 *Women and Family Health*. ISBN 81-7141- 497-4.

Vol. 5 *Women and International Action*. ISBN 81-7141-498-2.

Babu, P.C , author and Digumarti Bhaskara Rao, editor (2004). *Flowers of Wisdom*. New Delhi : Discovery Publishing House. ISBN 81-7141-695-0

Babu, P.C., author and Digumarti Bhaskara Rao, editor (2008). *Worlds of Wisdom*. New Delhi: Discovery Publishing House.

Bhagya Lakshmi, L., author and Digumarti Bhaskara Rao, editor (2000). *Reading and Comprehension*. New Delhi : Discovery Publishing House. ISBN 81-7141-543-1.

Bhasha, S.A., author and Digumarti Bhaskara Rao, editor (2004). *Methods of Teaching Geography*. New Delhi : Discovery Publishing House. ISBN 81-7141-807-4.

Bhaskara Rao, Digumarti (1986). *Dhrushya Sravana Bodhanapakaranalu* (Audio Visual Teaching Aids). Guntur : Nagarjuna Publishers.

Bhaskara Rao, Digumarti (1993). *Jeevasashtra Bodhana* (Teaching of Biology). Guntur : Nagarjuna Publishers.

Bhaskara Rao, Digumarti (1994). *Vidya Manovignana Sastram* (Educational Psychology). Guntur : Nagarjuna Publishers.

Bhaskara Rao, Digumarti (1995). *Vignanasasthra Bodhana* (Teaching of science) Guntur : Nagarjuna Publishers.

Bhaskara Rao, Digumarti (1997). *Vidya Manovignana Sastram* (Educational Psychology). Guntur : Creative Press.

Bhaskara Rao, Digumarti (1998). *DSC Study Material.* Guntur : Nagarjuna Publishers.

Bhaskara Rao, Digumarti (1998). *Upadhyayudu Vidya.* (Teacher and Education) Guntur : Nagarjuna Publishers.

Bhaskara Rao, Digumarti (1998). *Vidya Drukpadalu* (Perspectives of Education). Guntur : Nagarjuna Publishers.

Bhaskara Rao, Digumarti (1999). *EdCET Teaching Aptitude.* Guntur : Nagarjuna Publishers.

Bhaskara Rao, Digumarti (2001). *Bharata Samajamulo Upadyayudu Vidhya* (Teacher and Education in Emerging Indian Society). Guntur : Sri Nagarjuna Publishers.

Bhaskara Rao, Digumarti (2001). *Bhoutika Sastra Bodhana Padhatulu* (Methods of Teaching Physical Science). Guntur : Sri Nagarjuna Publishers.

Bhaskara Rao, Digumarti (2001). *Jeeva Sastra Bodhana Padhatulu* (Methods of Teaching Biology).Guntur : Sri Nagarjuna Publishers.

Bhaskara Rao, Digumarti (2001). *Vidya Manovignana Sastram* (Educational Psychology). Guntur : Sri Nagarjuna Publishers.

Bhaskara Rao, Digumarti (2003). *Patasala Yajamanyam / Paripalana* (School Management and Administration). Guntur : Sri Nagarjuna Publishers.

Bhaskara Rao, Digumarti and A. Jagadish (2009). *Vignansastra Bodhana Padhatulu* (Methods of Teaching Science).Guntur : Sri Nagarjuna Publishers.

Bhaskara Rao, Digumarti and B. Prasad Babu (2009). *Pradhamika Vidya mariyu Vileena Vidya Dhrukpadhalu* (Perspectives in Primary Education and Inclusive Education). Guntur : Sri Nagarjuna Publishers.

Bhaskara Rao, Digumarti and B. Prasad Babu (2009). *Vidya Manovignana Sastram* (Educational Psychology). Guntur : Sri Nagarjuna Publishers.

Bhaskara Rao, Digumarti and D. Naresh Kumar (2004). *School Teacher Effectiveness.* New Delhi : Discovery Publishing House. ISBN 81-7141-782-5.

Bhaskara Rao, Digumarti and Digumarthi Harshitha (2004). *Adjustment of Adolescents.* New Delhi: APH Publishing House. ISBN 81-7648-836-8.

Bhaskara Rao, Digumarti and Digumarthi Harshitha, editors (2001). *Education in India.* New Delhi: APH Publishing House. ISBN 81-7648-207-2.

Bhaskara Rao, Digumarti and Digumarti Pushpa Latha (1994). *Achievement in Biology*. New Delhi : Discovery Publishing House. ISBN 81-7141-264-5.

Bhaskara Rao, Digumarti and Digumarti Pushpa Latha (1994). *Achievement in Science*. New Delhi : Discovery Publishing House. ISBN 81-7141-280-70.

Bhaskara Rao, Digumarti and Digumarti Pushpa Latha (1995). *Achievement in English*. New Delhi : Discovery Publishing House. ISBN 81-7141-283-1.

Bhaskara Rao, Digumarti and Digumarti Pushpa Latha (1995). *Achievement in Mathematics*. New Delhi : Discovery Publishing House. ISBN 81-7141-278-5.

Bhaskara Rao, Digumarti and Digumarti Pushpa Latha (2004). *Education for Women*. New Delhi : Discovery Publishing House. ISBN 81-7141-873-2.

Bhaskara Rao, Digumarti and E. Sreekanth Babu (2004). *Educational Interests of School Students*. New Delhi : Discovery Publishing House. ISBN 81-7141-837-6.

Bhaskara Rao, Digumarti and G. Prasanthi (2009). *Samardya Nirmanamu* (Capacity Building). Guntur : Sri Nagarjuna Publishers.

Bhaskara Rao, Digumarti and K. Subba Rao (2009). *Elementary Vidya, Pranalika, Yajamanyam, Upadyaya Kartavyalu* (Elementary Education, Planning, Management and Teacher Functions). Guntur : Sri Nagarjuna Publishers.

Bhaskara Rao, Digumarti and K. Vijaya (1995). *A Text Book Evaluation*. Ambala Cantt : The Associated Publishers.

Bhaskara Rao, Digumarti and K.R.S. Sambasiva Rao, editors (1996). *Current Trends in Indian Education*. New Delhi : Discovery Publishing House. ISBN 81-7141-311-0.

Bhaskara Rao, Digumarti and M.A. Fayaz (2004). *Problems of Primary School Drop-outs*. New Delhi : Discovery Publishing House. ISBN 81-7141- 834-1.

Bhaskara Rao, Digumarti and N.V.M. Mohana Rao (2002). *Problems of Mentally Handicapped Children*. New Delhi : Discovery Publishing House. ISBN 81-7141- 645-4.

Bhaskara Rao, Digumarti and S. Chandra Mohan (2002). *Sports Management*. New Delhi : APH Publishing House. ISBN 81-7648-467-9.

Bhaskara Rao, Digumarti and S.A. Khader (2004). *Problems of Private School Teachers*. New Delhi : Discovery Publishing Corporation. ISBN 81-7141-838-4.

Bhaskara Rao, Digumarti and S.A. Khader (2004). *School Education in India.* New Delhi : Discovery Publishing Corporation. ISBN 81-7141-849-X.

Bhaskara Rao, Digumarti and Sk. Johni Basha (2004). *Teachers' Population Education Awareness.* New Delhi : Discovery Publishing House. ISBN 81-7141-832-5.

Bhaskara Rao, Digumarti, Digumarthi Harshitha and K.R.S. Sambasiva Rao, editors (1999). *Advanced Biotechnology.* New Delhi : Discovery Publishing House. ISBN 81-7141-516-4.

Bhaskara Rao, Digumarti, Digumarti Pushpa Latha and Digumarthi Harshitha, editors (2001). *Biological Warfare.* New Delhi: Discovery Publishing House. ISBN 81-7141-597-0.

Bhaskara Rao, Digumarti, Digumarti Pushpa Latha and Digumarthi Harshitha, editors (2001). *Women as Educators.* New Delhi: Discovery Publishing House. ISBN 81-7141-602-0.

Bhaskara Rao, Digumarti, Digumarti Pushpa Latha and Digumarthi Harshitha, editors (2001). *Assessing Learning Achievement.* New Delhi : Discovery Publishing House. ISBN 81-7141-601-2.

Bhaskara Rao, Digumarti, Digumarti Pushpa Latha and Digumarthi Harshitha, editors (2001). *Energy Security.* New Delhi : Discovery Publishing House. ISBN 81-7141-598-9.

Bhaskara Rao, Digumarti, Editor (2010). *Elementary Vidya, Pranalika, Yajamanyam, Upadyaya Kartavyalu – Question Bank* (Elementary Education, Planning, Management and Teacher Functions). Guntur: Sri Nagarjuna Publishers.

Bhaskara Rao, Digumarti, editor (2010). *Ganithasastra Bodhana Padhatulu – Question Bank* (Methods of Teaching Science).Guntur : Sri Nagarjuna Publishers.

Bhaskara Rao, Digumarti, editor (2010). *Methods of Teaching English – Question Bank.* Guntur : Sri Nagarjuna Publishers.

Bhaskara Rao, Digumarti, editor (2010). *Pradhamika Vidya mariyu Vileena Vidya Dhrukpadhalu – Question Bank* (Perspectives in Primary Education and Inclusive Education). Guntur : Sri Nagarjuna Publishers.

Bhaskara Rao, Digumarti, editor (2010). *Samardya Nirmanamu – Question Bank* (Capacity Building). Guntur : Sri Nagarjuna Publishers.

Bhaskara Rao, Digumarti, editor (2010). *Sanghikasastra Bodhana Padhatulu – Question Bank* (Methods of Teaching Social Studies).Guntur : Sri Nagarjuna Publishers.

Bhaskara Rao, Digumarti, editor (2010). *Telugu Bodhana Padhatulu – Question Bank* (Methods of Teaching Social Studies).Guntur : Sri Nagarjuna Publishers.

Bhaskara Rao, Digumarti, editor (2010). *Vidya Manovignana Sastram – Question Bank* (Educational Psychology). Guntur : Sri Nagarjuna Publishers.

Bhaskara Rao, Digumarti, editor (2010). *Vignansastra Bodhana Padhatulu – Question Bank* (Methods of Teaching Science).Guntur : Sri Nagarjuna Publishers.

Bhaskara Rao, Digumarti, N. Saraja, J. Lalitha and V. Mrunalini, Translators (2008). *Vidya – Samajam (Education - Society). Hyderabad* : Dr. B. R. Ambedkar Open University.

Bhaskara Rao, Digumarti, V.V. Rao, V.V. Lakshmi and V.V. Krishna, editors (1999). *Status and Advancement of Women.* New Delhi: APH Publishing Corporation. ISBN 81-7648-169-6.

Bhuvaneswara Lakshmi, G. and K. Subba Rao, authors and Digumarti Bhaskara Rao, editor (2004). *Methods of Teaching Biology.* New Delhi : Discovery Publishing House. ISBN 81-7141-914-3.

Bhuvaneswara Lakshmi, G., author and Digumarti Bhaskara Rao, editor (2004). *Methods of Teaching Life Science.* New Delhi : Discovery Publishing House. ISBN 81-7141-804-X.

Bhuvaneswara Lakshmi, Gadde, author and Digumarti Bhaskara Rao, editor(2000). *Attitude Towards Science.* New Delhi : Discovery Publishing House. ISBN 81-7141-541-6.

Bujji Babu, K., author and Digumarti Bhaskara Rao, editor (2007). *Teaching Aptitude of Primary School Teachers.* New Delhi: Sonali Publications. ISBN 81-8411-083-9.

Chary, K.V.N.B., author and Digumarti Bhaskara Rao, editor (2006). *Techniques of Teaching Physics.* New Delhi : Sonali Publications. ISBN 81-8411-046-4.

Chowdary, S.B.J.R. and Naga Raju, authors and Digumarti Bhaskara Rao, editor (2004). *Mastery of Teaching Skills.* New Delhi : Discovery Publishing House.

Dayakara Reddy, V. and Digumarti Bhaskara Rao, editors (2006). *Value-Oriented Education.* New Delhi : Discovery Publishing House.

Devraj, T.A.S., author and Digumarti Bhaskara Rao, editor (1997). *Trace Analysis of Uranium and Thorium.* New Delhi : Discovery Publishing House. ISBN 81-7141-375-7.

Digumarti Bhaskara Rao and M. Srihari (2009). *Vardamana Bharata Desamulo Vidya* (Education in Emerging India). Guntur : Sri Nagarjuna Publishers.

Digumarti Bhaskara Rao, editor (2010). *Vardamana Bharata Desamulo Vidya – Question Bank* (Education in Emerging India). Guntur : Sri Nagarjuna Publishers.

Durga Rani, K., author and Digumarti Bhaskara Rao, editor (2000). *Educational Aspirations and Scientific Attitudes.* New Delhi : Discovery Publishing House. ISBN 81-7141-555-5.

Dutt, B.S.V. and Digumarti Bhaskara Rao (2001). *Empowering Primary Teachers.* New Delhi : Discovery Publishing House. ISBN 81-7141-615-2.

Dutt, B.S.V., author and Digumarti Bhaskara Rao, editor (2004). *Comparative Education.* New Delhi: Discovery Publishing House. ISBN 81-7141-912-7.

Ediger, Marlow and Digumarti Bhaskara Rao (1996). *Science Curriculum.* New Delhi: Discovery Publishing House. ISBN 81-7141-321-8.

Ediger, Marlow and Digumarti Bhaskara Rao (2000). *Teaching Mathematics Successfully.* New Delhi : Discovery Publishing House. ISBN 81-7141-552-0.

Ediger, Marlow and Digumarti Bhaskara Rao (2001). *Teaching Science Successfully.* New Delhi : Discovery Publishing House. ISBN 81-7141-600-4.

Ediger, Marlow and Digumarti Bhaskara Rao (2001). *Teaching Social Studies Successfully.* New Delhi : Discovery Publishing House. ISBN 81-7141-596-2.

Ediger, Marlow and Digumarti Bhaskara Rao (2002). *Elementary Curriculum.* New Delhi : Discovery Publishing House. ISBN 81-7141-658-6.

Ediger, Marlow and Digumarti Bhaskara Rao (2002). *Improving School Administration.* New Delhi : Discovery Publishing House. ISBN 81-7141-633-0

Ediger, Marlow and Digumarti Bhaskara Rao (2002). *Philosophy and Curriculum.* New Delhi: Discovery Publishing House. ISBN 81-7141-631-4.

Ediger, Marlow and Digumarti Bhaskara Rao (2003). *Elementary Curriculum Improvement.* New Delhi : Discovery Publishing House. ISBN 81-7141-740-X.

Ediger, Marlow and Digumarti Bhaskara Rao (2003). *Language Arts Curriculum.* New Delhi : Discovery Publishing House. ISBN 81-7141-657-8.

Ediger, Marlow and Digumarti Bhaskara Rao (2003). *Psychology and Curriculum.* New Delhi : Discovery Publishing House. ISBN 81-7141-691-8.

Ediger, Marlow and Digumarti Bhaskara Rao (2003). *School Curriculum and Administration.* New Delhi : Discovery Publishing House. ISBN 81-7141-709-4.

Ediger, Marlow and Digumarti Bhaskara Rao (2003). *School Curriculum and Administration.* New Delhi : Discovery Publishing House. ISBN 81-7141-709-4.

Ediger, Marlow and Digumarti Bhaskara Rao (2003). *Teaching Language Arts Successfully.* New Delhi : Discovery Publishing House. ISBN 81-7141-

Ediger, Marlow and Digumarti Bhaskara Rao (2003). *Teaching Mathematics in Elementary Schools.* New Delhi : Discovery Publishing House. ISBN 81-7141-687-X.

Ediger, Marlow and Digumarti Bhaskara Rao (2003). *Teaching Science in Elementary Schools.* New Delhi: Discovery Publishing House. ISBN 81-7141-698-5.

Ediger, Marlow and Digumarti Bhaskara Rao (2004). *Relevancy in Elementary Curriculum.* New Delhi : Discovery Publishing House. ISBN 81-7141-845-9.

Ediger, Marlow and Digumarti Bhaskara Rao (2004). *School Organisation.* New Delhi : Discovery Publishing House. ISBN 81-7141-843-0.

Ediger, Marlow and Digumarti Bhaskara Rao (2005). *Quality School Education.* New Delhi : Discovery Publishing House. ISBN 81-8356-022-9.

Ediger, Marlow and Digumarti Bhaskara Rao (2006). *Administration of Schools.* New Delhi : Discovery Publishing House.

Ediger, Marlow and Digumarti Bhaskara Rao (2006). *Community College – Curriculum and Teaching.* New Delhi : Discovery Publishing House. ISBN 81-8356-053-9.

Ediger, Marlow and Digumarti Bhaskara Rao (2006). *Curriculum of School Subjects.* New Delhi : Discovery Publishing House.

Ediger, Marlow and Digumarti Bhaskara Rao (2006). *Curriculum Organisation.* New Delhi: Discovery Publishing House.

Ediger, Marlow and Digumarti Bhaskara Rao (2006). *Issues in School Curruculum.* New Delhi : Discovery Publishing House. ISBN 81-8356-052-0.

Ediger, Marlow and Digumarti Bhaskara Rao (2006). *Reading Curriculum and Instruction.* New Delhi : Discovery Publishing House.

Ediger, Marlow and Digumarti Bhaskara Rao (2006). *Successful School Education.* New Delhi : Discovery Publishing House. ISBN 81-8356-054-7.

Ediger, Marlow and Digumarti Bhaskara Rao (2006). *Successful School Administration.* New Delhi : Discovery Publishing House. ISBN 81-8356-046-6.

Ediger, Marlow and Digumarti Bhaskara Rao (2007). *Language Arts Education.* New Delhi : Discovery Publishing House. ISBN 81-8356-333-3.

Ediger, Marlow and Digumarti Bhaskara Rao (2007). *School Science Education.* New Delhi : Discovery Publishing House. ISBN 81-8356-352-X.

Ediger, Marlow and Digumarti Bhaskara Rao (2010). *Effective Schooling.* New Delhi : Discovery Publishing House. ISBN 978-81-8356-613-1.

Ediger, Marlow and Digumarti Bhaskara Rao (2010). *Effective School Curriculum.* New Delhi : Discovery Publishing House. ISBN 978-81-8356-585-1.

Ediger, Marlow and Digumarti Bhaskara Rao (2010). *Essays on Teaching Science.* New Delhi : Discovery Publishing House.

Ediger, Marlow and Digumarti Bhaskara Rao (2010). *Essays on Teaching Social Studies.* New Delhi : Discovery Publishing House.

Ediger, Marlow and Digumarti Bhaskara Rao (2010). *Essays on Teaching Reading.* New Delhi : Discovery Publishing House.

Ediger, Marlow and Digumarti Bhaskara Rao (2010). *Essays on Teaching Mathematics.* New Delhi : Discovery Publishing House.

Ediger, Marlow and Digumarti Bhaskara Rao (2010). *Essays on Teaching and Learning.* New Delhi : Discovery Publishing House.

Ediger, Marlow and Digumarti Bhaskara Rao, editors (2006). *Encyclopaedia of School Education*, 5 volumes. New Delhi : Discovery Publishing House. ISBN 81-8356-308-2 (set).

Ediger, Marlow and Digumarti Bhaskara Rao, editors (2006). *Encyclopaedia of School Administration*, 4 volumes. New Delhi : Discovery Publishing House. ISBN 81-8356-307-4 (set).

Ediger, Marlow and Digumarti Bhaskara Rao, editors (2007). *Encyclopaedia of School Curriculum*, 10 volumes. New Delhi : Discovery Publishing House. ISBN 81-8356-305-8 (set).

Ediger, Marlow and Digumarti Bhaskara Rao, editors (2007). *Encyclopaedia of Teaching*, 8 volumes. New Delhi : Discovery Publishing House. ISBN 81-8356-305-8 (set).

Ediger, Marlow, B.S.V. Dutt and Digumarti Bhaskara Rao (2003). *Teaching English Successfully.* New Delhi : Discovery Publishing House. ISBN 81-7141-707-8.

Elizabeth, M.E.S., author and Digumarti Bhaskara Rao, editor (2004). *Methods of Teaching English.* New Delhi : Discovery Publishing House. ISBN 81-7141-809-0.

Elizabeth, M.E.S., author and Digumarti Bhaskara Rao, editor (2004). *Acquisition of English Vocabulary.* New Delhi : Discovery Publishing House. ISBN 81-7141- .

Fatima, Sk. and Digumarti Bhaskara Rao (2008). *Reasoning Ability of Adolescent Students.* New Delhi : Sonali Publications.

Fatima, Sk. author and Digumarti Bhaskara Rao, editor (2007). *Reasoning Ability of School Students.* New Delhi : Discovery Publishing House. ISBN 81-8356-330-9.

G.E.P. Sastry and G. Satya Narayana, authors, Bhaskara Rao, Digumarti, editor (2009). *Sanghikasastra Bodhana Padhatulu* (Methods of Teaching Social Studies).Guntur : Sri Nagarjuna Publishers.

Gopala Krishna, G., A. Rama Krishna, K. Subba Rao and Bhaskara Rao, Digumarti (2004). *Jeevasashtra Bodhana Padhatulu* (Methods of Teaching of Biological science). Guntur : Sri Nagarjuna Publishers.

Gopala Krishna, M., author and Digumarti Bhaskara Rao, editor (2007). *Techniques of Teaching Physical Education.* New Delhi : Sonali Publications. ISBN 81-8411-044-8.

Gopala Krishna, M., author and Digumarti Bhaskara Rao, editor (2007). *Techniques of Teaching Education.* New Delhi : Sonali Publications. ISBN 81-8411-062-6.

Harshitha, Digumarthi, author and Digumarti Bhaskara Rao, editor (2004). *Methods of Teaching Information Technology.* New Delhi : Discovery Publishing House. ISBN 81-7141-805-8.

Harshitha, Digumarthi, author and Digumarti Bhaskara Rao, editor (2007). *Techniques of Teaching Computer Science.* New Delhi : Sonali Publications. ISBN 81-8411-036-7.

Indira Devi, author and J. Prasanth Kumar and Digumarti Bhaskara Rao, editors (2004). *Values in Language Text Books.* New Delhi : APH Publishing Corporation. ISBN 81-7648-

Jalaja Kumari, C., author and Digumarti Bhaskara Rao, editor (2004). *Methods of Teaching Educational Technology.* New Delhi : Discovery Publishing House. ISBN 81-7141-810-4.

Jalaja Kumari, C., author and Digumarti Bhaskara Rao, editor (2007). *Job Satisfaction of Teachers.* New Delhi : Discovery Publishing House.

Janardhan Reddy, B., author and Digumarti Bhaskara Rao, editor (2006). *Techniques of Teaching Sociology.* New Delhi : Sonali Publications. ISBN 81-8411-042-1.

Jayasree, K., author and Digumarti Bhaskara Rao, editor (1999). *Correlates of Socialisation.* New Delhi : Discovery Publishing House. ISBN 81-7141-517-2.

Jayasree, K., author and Digumarti Bhaskara Rao, editor (2004). *Methods of Teaching Science.* New Delhi : Discovery Publishing House. ISBN 81-7141-801-5.

John Babu, C., author and T.J.R. Prasad, G.M. Madhukar and Digumarti Bhaskara Rao, editors (2004). *Problem Solving in Mathematics.* New Delhi : APH Publishing Corporation. ISBN 81-7648-273-0.

Joseph Raju, B and G.A. Anitha, authors and Digumarti Bhaskara Rao, editor (2004). *Population Education.* New Delhi : Sonali Publications. ISBN 81-88836-31-3.

Krishna Murthy, V., K.S. Sudheer Reddy and Digumarti Bhaskara Rao (2004). *Vidya Manovignana Sastra Adharalu* (Foundations of Educational Psychology). Guntur : Sri Nagarjuna Publishers.

Krishna, G., author and Digumarti Bhaskara Rao, editor (2006). *Techniques of Teaching Physical Education.* New Delhi : Discovery Publishing House. ISBN 81-8411-044-8.

Kumar Raja, G., author and Digumarti Bhaskara Rao, editor (2007). *Principles of Primary School.* New Delhi : Sonali Publications. ISBN 81-8411-054-5.

Lakshmi Kumari, V., author and Digumarti Bhaskara Rao, editor (2006). *Techniques of Teaching Home Science.* New Delhi : Discovery Publishing House. ISBN 81-8411-048-0.

Lalini, V., V. Dayakara Reddy, M. Srihari and Digumarti Bhaskara Rao (2004). *Vidya Adharalu* (Foundations of Education). Guntur : Sri Nagarjuna Publishers.

Lalitha, T., author and K.S. Prabhakaram, D.S.N. Sastry and Digumarti Bhaskara Rao, editors (2004). *Educational Philosophic Beliefs.* New Delhi: Discovery Publishing House. ISBN 81-7141-765-5.

Madhava, K., author and Digumarti Bhaskara Rao, editor (2008). *Personality of Adolescent Students.* New Delhi: Sonali Publications.

Madhu Bala, Jampala, author and Digumarti Bhaskara Rao, editor (2004). *Methods of Teaching Exceptional Children.* New Delhi: Discovery Publishing House. ISBN 81-7141-802-3.

Madhu Bala, Jampala, author and Digumarti Bhaskara Rao, editor (2007). *Adjustment, Achievement Motivation and Academic Achievement of Hearing Impaired Students.* New Delhi: Discovery Publishing House

Marja, Talvi and Digumarti Bhaskara Rao, editors (1996). *Educational Leadership and Social Changes.* New Delhi : Discovery Publishing House. ISBN 81-7141-320-X.

Marlow Ediger and Digumarti Bhaskara Rao, editors (2006). *Encyclopaedia of School Education*, 5 volumes. New Delhi : Discovery Publishing House. ISBN 81-8356-308-2 (set).

Marlow Ediger and Digumarti Bhaskara Rao, editors (2006). *Encyclopaedia of School Administration*, 4 volumes. New Delhi : Discovery Publishing House. ISBN 81-8356-307-4 (set).

Marlow Ediger and Digumarti Bhaskara Rao, editors (2007). *Encyclopaedia of School Curriculum*, 10 volumes. New Delhi : Discovery Publishing House. ISBN 81-8356-305-8 (set).

Marlow Ediger and Digumarti Bhaskara Rao, editors (2007). *Encyclopaedia of Teaching*, 8 volumes. New Delhi : Discovery Publishing House. ISBN 81-8356-305-8 (set).

Naga Kumari, U., author and Digumarti Bhaskara Rao, editor (2008). *Science Process Skills of School Students*. New Delhi : Sonali Publications.

Nageswara Rao, S. and M. Srihari, authors and Digumarti Bhaskara Rao, editor (2004). *Guidance and Counselling*. New Delhi : Discovery Publishing House. ISBN 81-7141-840-6.

Nageswara Rao, S. and P. Sridhar, authors and Digumarti Bhaskara Rao, editor (2004). *Methods and Techniques of Teaching*. New Delhi : Sonali Publications. ISBN 81-88836-33-8.

Nageswara Rao, S., author and Digumarti Bhaskara Rao, editor (2006). *Techniques of Teaching Psychology*. New Delhi : Discovery Publishing House. ISBN 81-8411-040-5.

Nirmala Jyothi, M., author and Digumarti Bhaskara Rao, editor (2003). *Non-detention System in School Education*. New Delhi : Discovery Publishing House. ISBN 81-7141-654-3.

Padma Tulasi, G., author and Digumarti Bhaskara Rao, editor (2004). *Methods of Teaching Elementary Science*. New Delhi : Discovery Publishing House. ISBN 81-7141-871-6.

Pala Prasada Rao, V., author and D. Bhaskara Rao, editors (2008). *Functioning of Autonomous Colleges*. New Delhi : Sonali Publications.

Pala Prasada Rao, V., author and K. N. Rani and D. Bhaskara Rao, editors (2004).*India Pakistan : Partition Perspectives in Indo English Novels*. New Delhi: Discovery Publishing House. ISBN 81-7141-871-6.

Pitchi Reddy, M., author and Digumarti Bhaskara Rao, editor (2007). *Techniques of Teaching Social Sciences*. New Delhi : Sonali Publications. ISBN 81-8411-066-X.

Prabhakaram, K.S., author and Digumarti Bhaskara Rao, editors (1998). *Concept Attainment Model in Mathematics Teaching*. New Delhi : Discovery Publishing House. ISBN 81-7141-424-9.

Prasad Babu, B., author and M.V.R. Raju and Digumarti Bhaskara Rao, editors (2006). *Behavioural Problems of School Children*. New Delhi: Discovery Publishing House. ISBN 81-8356-206-X.

Prasad Babu, B., author and P. Madhu and Digumarti Bhaskara Rao, editors (2006). *Psychological Adjustment and Well-being*. New Delhi: Discovery Publishing House. ISBN 81-8356-204-3.

Prasanth Kumar, J., author and Digumarti Bhaskara Rao, editor (1998). *Effectiveness of Distance Education System*. New Delhi : Discovery Publishing House. ISBN 81-7141-437-0.

Prasanth Kumar, J., author and Digumarti Bhaskara Rao, editor (2004). *Methods of Teaching Civics*. New Delhi : Discovery Publishing House. ISBN 81-7141-806-6.

Prasanth Kumar, J., author and G. Sundara Rao and Digumarti Bhaskara Rao, editors (2000). *Open University Student Support Services*. New Delhi : Discovery Publishing House. ISBN 81-7141-550-4.

Raja Kumari, M.A. and D.R.S. Sundari, authors and Digumarti Bhaskara Rao, editor (2004). *Special Education*. New Delhi : Discovery Publishing House. ISBN 81-7141-846-5.

Raja Kumari, M.A. and D.R.S. Sundari, authors and Digumarti Bhaskara Rao, editor (2004). *Methods of Teaching Educational Psychology*. New Delhi : Discovery Publishing House. ISBN 81-7141-

Rama Krishna Prasad and P. Vide Sagar, authors and Digumarti Bhaskara Rao, editor (2004). *Methods of Teaching Physical Education*. New Delhi: Discovery Publishing House.

Rama Krishnaiah, D., author and Digumarti Bhaskara Rao, editor (1998). *Job Satisfaction of College Teachers*. New Delhi : Discovery Publishing House. ISBN 81-7141-438-9.

Rama Kumar Ratnam, M.V., author and Digumarti Bhaskara Rao, editor (1998). *Dukkha : Suffering in Early Buddhism*. New Delhi: Discovery Publishing House. ISBN 81-7141-653-5.

Rama Seshaiah, P. author and Digumarti Bhaskara Rao, editor (2004). *Methods of Teaching Home Science*. New Delhi : Discovery Publishing House. ISBN 81-7141-916-X.

Rama Swamy, K., author and Digumarti Bhaskara Rao, editor (2007). *Techniques of Teaching Environmental Science*. New Delhi : Sonali Publications. ISBN 81-8411-035-9.

Ramatulasamma, K., author and Digumarti Bhaskara Rao, editor (2002). *Job Satisfaction of Teacher Educators.* New Delhi : Discovery Publishing House. ISBN 81-7141-655-1.

Ramesh, A.R., author and Digumarti Bhaskara Rao, editor (2006). *Techniques of Teaching Commerce.* New Delhi : Sonali Publications. ISBN 81-8411-043-X.

Ramesh, Ghanta and Digumarti Bhaskara Rao, editors (1998). *Environmental Education : Problems and Prospects.* New Delhi: Discovery Publishing House. ISBN 81-7141-423-0.

Ranga Rao, B., author and Digumarti Bhaskara Rao, editor (2007). *Techniques of Teaching Economics.* New Delhi : Sonali Publications. ISBN 81-8411-056-1..

Ranga Rao, R., author and Digumarti Bhaskara Rao, editor (2004). *Methods of Teacher Teaching.* New Delhi : Discovery Publishing House. ISBN 81-7141-812-0.

Rani, S.S., author and Digumarti Bhaskara Rao, editor (2006). *Techniques of Teaching Botany.* New Delhi : Discovery Publishing House. ISBN 81-8411-037-5.

Rathaiah, Lavu and Digumarti Bhaskara Rao (1997). *Achievement Correlates.* New Delhi: Discovery Publishing House. ISBN 81-7141-385-4.

Rathaiah, Lavu and Digumarti Bhaskara Rao, editors (1996), *International Innovations in Education.* New Delhi : Discovery Publishing House. ISBN 81-7141-359-5.

Ravi Krishna, M., author and Digumarti Bhaskara Rao, editor (2004). *Examination System.* New Delhi : Discovery Publishing House. ISBN 81-7141-824-4.

Ravi Kumar, M., author and Digumarti Bhaskara Rao, editor (2004). *Methods of Teaching Computer Science.* New Delhi : Discovery Publishing House. ISBN 81-7141-823-6.

Rudramamba, B. and V. Lakshmi Kumari, authors and Digumarti Bhaskara Rao, editor (2004). *Methods of Teaching Economics.* New Delhi : Discovery Publishing House. ISBN 81-7141-900-3.

Rudramamba, B., author and Digumarti Bhaskara Rao, editor (2003). *Problems of Teaching.* New Delhi : APH Publishing Corporation. ISBN 81-7648-462-8.

Sambasiva Rao, P., author and Digumarti Bhaskara Rao, editor (2007). *Techniques of Teaching Psychology.* New Delhi : Sonali Publications. ISBN 81-8411-040-5.

Sanjeeva Rao, P.C., author and Digumarti Bhaskara Rao, editor (1996). *A Text Book of Geology.* New Delhi : Discovery Publishing House. ISBN 81-7141-313-7.

Santhanam, T., B. Prasad Babu and S. Sugandhi, authors and Digumarti Bhaskara Rao, editor (2007). *Children with Learning Disabilities.* New Delhi : Sonali Publications. ISBN 81-8411-077-4.

Santhanam, T., B. Prasad Babu and S. Sugandhi, authors and Digumarti Bhaskara Rao, editor (2008). *Learning Disabilities and Remedial Programmes.* New Delhi : Discovery Publishing House.

Sarala, M.M.O., author and Digumarti Bhaskara Rao, editor (2006). *Techniques of Teaching English.* New Delhi : Sonali Publications. ISBN 81-8411-047-2.

Satya Narayana, G., author and Digumarti Bhaskara Rao, editor (2008). *Attitude towards Social Studies and Achievement in Social Studies.* New Delhi : Sonali Publications.

Satya Narayana, P.V.V. and G. Krishna, authors and Digumarti Bhaskara Rao, editor (2004). *Curriculum Development and Management.* New Delhi : Discovery Publishing House. ISBN 81-7141-813-9.

Satya Narayana, V., author and Digumarti Bhaskara Rao, editor (2001). *Physical Education, Social Attitudes and Leadership Qualities.* New Delhi: Discovery Publishing House. ISBN 81-7141-593-8.

Shamsuddin, Sk. and V. Dayakara Reddy, authors and Digumarti Bhaskara Rao, editor (2007). *Academic Achievement and Values.* New Delhi : Discovery Publishing House.

Singh, Y.C., author and Digumarti Bhaskara Rao, editor (2006). *Techniques of Teaching Science.* New Delhi : Sonali Publications. ISBN 81-8411-041-3.

Sirisha Rani, S., author and Digumarti Bhaskara Rao, editor (2007). *Techniques of Teaching Botany.* New Delhi : Sonali Publications. ISBN 81-8411-037-5.

Siva Lakshmi, G.V. and G.L. Subbaiah, authors and Digumarti Bhaskara Rao, editor (2004). *Methods of Teaching Environmental Science.* New Delhi: Discovery Publishing House. ISBN 81-7141-839-2.

Sivaratnam Reddy, M., author and Digumarti Bhaskara Rao, editor (2004). *Creativity in College Students.* New Delhi : Discovery Publishing House. ISBN 81-7141-697-7.

Srihari, M., author and Digumarti Bhaskara Rao, editor (2003). *Values of Prospective Teachers.* New Delhi : Discovery Publishing House. ISBN 81-8356-328-7.

Srinivas Rao, P., author and Digumarti Bhaskara Rao, editor (2007). *Principles of Secondary School.* New Delhi : Sonali Publications. ISBN 81-8411-058-8.

Srinivas, G. and Digumarti Bhaskara Rao (2007). *Anxiety of Prospective Teachers.* New Delhi : Sonali Publications. ISBN 81-8411-084-7.

Srinivas, M. and I. Prasada Rao, authors and Digumarti Bhaskara Rao, editor (2004). *Methods of Teaching History.* New Delhi : Discovery Publishing House. ISBN 81-7141-

Srinivasa Rao, Mandalapu, author and Digumarti Bhaskara Rao, editor (2003). *Achievement Motivation and Achievement in Mathematics.* New Delhi : Discovery Publishing House. ISBN 81-7141-674-8.

Srinivasulu Reddy, M. and K.R.S. Sambasiva Rao, authors and Digumarti Bhaskara Rao, editor (1999). *A Text Book of Aquaculture.* New Delhi : Discovery Publishing House. ISBN 81-7141-482-6.

Subba Rao, K., author and Digumarti Bhaskara Rao, editor (2007). *School Education Policy.* New Delhi : Discovery Publishing House. ISBN 81-8356-285-X.

Subba Rao, K., author and Digumarti Bhaskara Rao, editor (2007). *Education Planning.* New Delhi : Sonali Publications. ISBN 81-8411-053-7.

Subba Rao, K.P., P. Ayodhya and Digumarti Bhaskara Rao (2004). *Patasala Yajamanyam – Vidhya Vyavasthalu* (School Management and Systems of Education). Guntur : Sri Nagarjuna Publishers.

Sudhakar Reddy, Y., author and Digumarti Bhaskara Rao, editor (2003). *Creativity in Adolescents.* New Delhi : Discovery Publishing House. ISBN 81-7141-659-4.

Sudhakar, V., B. Ravindra Babu, D.S. Kumar and Digumarti Bhaskara Rao (2004). *Vidya Sanketika Sastram - Computer Vidhya* (Educational Technology and Computer Education). Guntur : Sri Nagarjuna Publishers.

Suneetha, G., author and Digumarti Bhaskara Rao, editor (2004). *Environmental Awareness of School Students.* New Delhi : Sonali Publications. ISBN 81-8411-085-5.

Sunil Kumar, K. and K. Rama Krishana, authors and Digumarti Bhaskara Rao, editor (2004). *Methods of Teaching Chemistry.* New Delhi : Discovery Publishing House. ISBN 81-7141-913-5.

Sunita, E. and R. Sambasiva Rao, authors and Digumarti Bhaskara Rao, editor (2004). *Methods of Teaching Mathematics.* New Delhi : Discovery Publishing House. ISBN 81-7141-915-1.

Surya Madhava, I., author and Digumarti Bhaskara Rao, editor (2006). *Techniques of Teaching Geography.* New Delhi : Discovery Publishing House. ISBN 81-8411-034-0.

Surya Madhava, I., author and Digumarti Bhaskara Rao, editor (2007). *Techniques of Teaching Political Science.* New Delhi : Discovery Publishing House. ISBN 81-8411-061-8.

Swamy, K.R., author and Digumarti Bhaskara Rao, editor (2006). *Techniques of Teaching Environmental Science.* New Delhi : Discovery Publishing House. ISBN 81-8411-035-9.

Swarna Jyothi, K., author and Digumarti Bhaskara Rao, editor (2007). *Educational Research.* New Delhi : Sonali Publications. ISBN 81-8411-063-4.

Swarna Latha, C.D., and Digumarti Bhaskara Rao, editors (2006). *Encyclopaedia of Biotechnology,* 5 volumes. New Delhi : Discovery Publishing House. ISBN 81-8356-168-3.

Swarupa Rani, T. and J.R. Priyadarshini, authors and Digumarti Bhaskara Rao, editor (2004). *Educational Measurement and Evaluation.* New Delhi: Discovery Publishing House. ISBN 81-7141-859-7.

Valeri V. Koustiouk, author and Digumarti Bhaskara Rao, editor (2002). *A Text Book of Cryogenics.* New Delhi : Discovery Publishing House. ISBN 81-7141-642-X.

Vamsi Krishna, V., author and Digumarti Bhaskara Rao, editor (2004). *School Psychology.* New Delhi: Discovery Publishing House. ISBN 81-7141-880-5.

Vanaja, M. and N. Sneha Latha, authors and Digumarti Bhaskara Rao, editor (2004). *Student Shyness.* New Delhi : APH Publishing Corporation. ISBN 81-7648-

Vanaja, M., author and Digumarti Bhaskara Rao, editor (1999). *Inquiry Training Model.* New Delhi : Discovery Publishing House. ISBN 81-7141-515-6.

Vanaja, M., author and Digumarti Bhaskara Rao, editor (2004). *Methods of Teaching Physics.* New Delhi : Discovery Publishing House. ISBN 81-7141-867-8

Veena Kumari, Balusu and Digumarti Bhaskara Rao (1996). *Operation Black Board.* New Delhi : APH Publishing Corporation. ISBN 81-7024-711-X.

Veena Kumari, Balusu, author and Digumarti Bhaskara Rao, editor (2004). *Methods of Teaching Social Studies.* New Delhi : Discovery Publishing House. ISBN 81-7141-899-6.

Veena Kumari, Balusu, author and Digumarti Bhaskara Rao, editor (2000). *Psycho-Social Correlates of Achievement.* New Delhi : Discovery Publishing House. ISBN 81-7141-547-4.

Venkata Rao, B., author and Digumarti Bhaskara Rao, editor (2007). *Techniques of Teaching Chemistry.* New Delhi : Sonali Publications. ISBN 81-8411-057-X.

Venkata Rao, P. and Digumarti Bhaskara Rao (1989). *A Text Book of Zoology – Junior Intermediate.* Guntur : Vignan Publishers.

Venkata Rao, P. and Digumarti Bhaskara Rao (1989). *A Text Book of Zoology – Senior Intermediate.* Guntur : Vignan Publishers.

Venkateswara Rao, V., author and Digumarti Bhaskara Rao, editor (2004). *Problems of Education.* New Delhi : Discovery Publishing House. ISBN 81-7141-841-4.

Venkateswara Rao, V., V. Vijaya Lakshmi and V. Vamsi Krishna, authors and Digumarti Bhaskara Rao, editor (2004). *Education For All.* New Delhi : Sonali Publications. ISBN 81-88836-30-3.

Venkateswara Rao, V., V. Vijaya Lakshmi and V. Vamsi Krishna, authors and Digumarti Bhaskara Rao, editor (2004). *Education in India.* New Delhi : Sonali Publications. ISBN 81-88836-858-9.

Venkateswara Reddy, L. and Narayana, M. L, authors and Digumarti Bhaskara Rao, editor (2004). *Methods of Teaching Rural Sociology.* New Delhi : Discovery Publishing House. ISBN 81-7141-811-2.

Venkateswara Reddy, L. and Narayana, M. L., authors and Digumarti Bhaskara Rao, editor (2004). *Education for Dalits.* New Delhi : Discovery Publishing House. ISBN 81-7141-872-4.

Venkateswarlu, K. and S.J. Basha, authors and Digumarti Bhaskara Rao, editor (2004). *Methods of Teaching Commerce.* New Delhi : Discovery Publishing House. ISBN 81-7141-808-2.

Venugopala Rao, K., author and Digumarti Bhaskara Rao, editor (2000). *Teacher Morale in Secondary Schools.* New Delhi : Discovery Publishing House. ISBN 81-7141-551-2.

Venugopala Rao, K., author and Digumarti Bhaskara Rao, editor (2007). *Techniques of Teaching history.* New Delhi : Sonali Publications. ISBN 81-8411-059-6.

Vidya, C., author and Digumarti Bhaskara Rao, editor (1996). *A Text Book of Nutrition.* New Delhi : Discovery Publishing House. ISBN 81-7141-309-9.

Vijaya Bharathi, D., author and Digumarti Bhaskara Rao, editor (2000). *Educational Philosophies of Swami Vivekananda and John Dewey.* New Delhi : APH Publishing House. ISBN 81-7648-309-9.

Vijaya Bharathi, D., author and Digumarti Bhaskara Rao, editor (2005). *Educational Philosophy of John Dewey.* New Delhi : Discovery Publishing House. ISBN 81-8356-024-5.

Vijaya Bharathi, D., author and Digumarti Bhaskara Rao, editor (2005). *Educational Philosophy of Swami Vivekananda.* New Delhi : Discovery Publishing House. ISBN 81-8356-023-7.

Vijaya Kumar, S.J., author and Digumarti Bhaskara Rao, editor (2006). *Techniques of Teaching Mathematics.* New Delhi : Sonali Publications. ISBN 81-8411-039-1.

Vijaya Lakshmi, D., author and Digumarti Bhaskara Rao, editor (2004) *Basic Education.* New Delhi : Discovery Publishing House. ISBN 81-7141-881-3.

Vijaya Lakshmi, V., author and Digumarti Bhaskara Rao, editor (2006). *Techniques of Teaching Music.* New Delhi : Discovery Publishing House. ISBN 81-8411-038-3.

Vimala, T.D., B. Prasad Babu and Digumarti Bhaskara Rao, editors (2007). *Stress, Coping and Management.* New Delhi : Sonali Publications. ISBN 81-8411-086-3.

Visalakshi, V., author and Digumarti Bhaskara Rao, editor (2006). *Techniques of Teaching Biology.* New Delhi : Sonali Publications. ISBN 81-8411-045-6.

Visalakshi, V., author and Digumarti Bhaskara Rao, editor (2007). *Techniques of Teaching Zoology.* New Delhi : Sonali Publications. ISBN 81-8411-055-3.

Index

D

E

K

L

M